JULIUS CAESAR

William Shakespeare

COLLINS
CL

Harper Press
An imprint of HarperCollins*Publishers*
77–85 Fulham Palace Road
Hammersmith
London W6 8JB

This Harper Press paperback edition published 2011

A catalogue record for this book is available from the British Library

ISBN: 978-0-00-792546-9

Printed and bound in Great Britain by Clays Ltd, St Ives plc

MIX
Paper from
responsible sources
FSC™ C007454

FSC™ is a non-profit international organisation established to promote
the responsible management of the world's forests. Products carrying the
FSC label are independently certified to assure consumers that they come
from forests that are managed to meet the social, economic and
ecological needs of present and future generations,
and other controlled sources.

Find out more about HarperCollins and the environment at
www.harpercollins.co.uk/green

Life & Times section © Gerard Cheshire
Introduction by Patrick Reilly
Shakespeare: Words and Phrases adapted from
Collins English Dictionary
Typesetting in Kalix by Palimpsest Book Production Limited,
Falkirk, Stirlingshire

10 9 8 7 6 5 4 3 2 1

Prefatory Note

This Shakespeare play uses the full Alexander text. By keeping in mind the fact that the language has changed considerably in four hundred years, as have customs, jokes, and stage conventions, the editors have aimed at helping the modern reader – whether English is their mother tongue or not – to grasp the full significance of the play. The Notes, intended primarily for examination candidates, are presented in a simple, direct style. The needs of those unfamiliar with British culture have been specially considered.

Since quiet study of the printed word is unlikely to bring fully to life plays that were written directly for the public theatre, attention has been drawn to dramatic effects which are important in performance. The editors see Shakespeare's plays as living works of art which can be enjoyed today on stage, film and television in many parts of the world.

CONTENTS

An Elizabethan playhouse. Note the apron stage protruding into the auditorium, the space below it, the inner room at the rear of the stage, the gallery above the inner stage, the canopy over the main stage, and the absence of a roof over the audience.

The Theatre in
Shakespeare's Day

On the face of it, the conditions in the Elizabethan theatre were not such as to encourage great writers. The public playhouse itself was not very different from an ordinary inn-yard; it was open to the weather; among the spectators were often louts, pickpockets and prostitutes; some of the actors played up to the rowdy elements in the audience by inserting their own jokes into the authors' lines, while others spoke their words loudly but unfeelingly; the presentation was often rough and noisy, with fireworks to represent storms and battles, and a table and a few chairs to represent a tavern; there were no actresses, so boys took the parts of women, even such subtle and mature ones as Cleopatra and Lady Macbeth; there was rarely any scenery at all in the modern sense. In fact, a quick inspection of the English theatre in the reign of Elizabeth I by a time-traveller from the twentieth century might well produce only one positive reaction: the costumes were often elaborate and beautiful.

Shakespeare himself makes frequent comments in his plays about the limitations of the playhouse and the actors of his time, often apologizing for them. At the beginning of *Henry V* the Prologue refers to the stage as 'this unworthy scaffold' and to the theatre building (the Globe, probably) as 'this wooden O', and emphasizes the urgent need for imagination in making up for all the deficiencies of presentation. In introducing Act IV the Chorus goes so far as to say:

> . . . we shall much disgrace
> With four or five most vile and ragged foils,
> Right ill-dispos'd in brawl ridiculous,
> The name of Agincourt, (lines 49–52)

In *A Midsummer Night's Dream* (Act V, Scene i) he seems to dismiss actors with the words:

The best in this kind are but shadows.

Yet Elizabeth's theatre, with all its faults, stimulated dramatists to a variety of achievement that has never been equalled and, in Shakespeare, produced one of the greatest writers in history. In spite of all his grumbles he seems to have been fascinated by the challenge that it presented him with. It is necessary to re-examine his theatre carefully in order to understand how he was able to achieve so much with the materials he chose to use. What sort of place was the Elizabethan playhouse in reality? What sort of people were these criticized actors? And what sort of audiences gave them their living?

The Development of the Theatre up to Shakespeare's Time

For centuries in England noblemen had employed groups of skilled people to entertain them when required. Under Tudor rule, as England became more secure and united, actors such as these were given more freedom, and they often performed in public, while still acknowledging their 'overlords' (in the 1570s, for example, when Shakespeare was still a schoolboy at Stratford, one famous company was called 'Lord Leicester's Men'). London was rapidly becoming larger and more important in the second half of the sixteenth century, and many of the companies of actors took the opportunities offered to establish themselves at inns on the main roads leading to the City (for example, the Boar's Head in Whitechapel and the Tabard in South-wark) or in the City itself. These groups of actors would come to an agreement with the inn-keeper which would give them the use of the yard for their performances after people had eaten and drunk well in the middle of the day. Before long, some inns were taken over completely by companies of players and thus became the first public theatres. In 1574 the officials of the City of London issued an order which shows clearly that these theatres were both popular and also offensive to some respectable people, because the order complains about 'the inordinate haunting of great multitudes of people, specially youth, to plays interludes and shows; namely occasion of frays and quarrels, evil practices of incontinency in great inns . . .' There is evidence that, on public holidays, the theatres on the banks of the Thames were crowded with noisy apprentices and tradesmen, but it would be wrong to think that audiences were always undiscriminating and loudmouthed. In spite of the disapproval of Puritans and the more staid members of society, by the 1590s, when Shakespeare's plays were beginning to be performed, audiences consisted of a good cross-section of English society, nobility as well as workers, intellectuals as well as simple people out for a laugh; also (and in this respect English theatres were unique in Europe), it was quite normal for respectable women to attend plays. So Shakespeare had to write plays which would appeal to people of widely different kinds. He had to provide 'something for everyone' but at the same time to take care to unify the material so that it would not seem to fall into separate pieces as they watched it. A speech like that of the drunken porter in *Macbeth* could provide the 'groundlings' with a belly-laugh, but also held a deeper significance for those who could appreciate it. The audience he wrote for was one of a number of apparent drawbacks which Shakespeare was able to turn to his and our advantage.

Shakespeare's Actors

Nor were all the actors of the time mere 'rogues, vagabonds and sturdy beggars' as some were described in a Statute of 1572. It is true that many of them had a hard life and earned very little money, but leading actors could become partners in the ownership of the theatres in which they acted: Shakespeare was a shareholder in the Globe and the Blackfriars theatres when he was an actor as well as a playwright. In any case, the attacks made on Elizabethan actors were usually directed at their morals and not at their acting ability; it is clear that many of them must have been good at their trade if they were able to interpret complex works like the great tragedies in such a way as to attract enthusiastic audiences. Undoubtedly some of the boys took the women's parts with skill and confidence, since a man called Coryate, visiting Venice in 1611, expressed surprise that women could act as well as they: 'I saw women act, a thing that I never saw before . . . and they performed it with as good a grace, action, gesture . . . as ever I saw any masculine actor.' The quality of most of the actors who first presented Shakespeare's plays is probably accurately summed up by Fynes Moryson, who wrote, '. . . as there be, in my opinion, more plays in London than in all the parts of the world I have seen, so do these players or comedians excel all other in the world.'

The Structure of the Public Theatre

Although the 'purpose-built' theatres were based on the inn-yards which had been used for play-acting, most of them were circular. The walls contained galleries on three storeys from which the wealthier patrons watched, they must have been something like the 'boxes' in a modern theatre, except that they held much larger numbers – as many as 1500. The 'groundlings' stood on the floor of the building, facing a raised stage which projected from the 'stage-wall', the main features of which were:

1 a small room opening on to the back of the main stage and on the same level as it (rear stage),
2 a gallery above this inner stage (upper stage),
3 canopy projecting from above the gallery over the main stage, to protect the actors from the weather (the 700 or 800 members of the audience who occupied the yard, or 'pit' as we call it today, had the sky above them).

In addition to these features there were dressing-rooms behind the stage and a space underneath it from which entrances could be made through trap-doors. All the acting areas – main stage, rear stage, upper stage and under stage – could be entered by actors directly from their dressing rooms, and all of them were used in productions of Shakespeare's plays. For example, the inner stage, an almost cavelike structure, would have been where Ferdinand and Miranda are 'discovered' playing chess in the last act of *The Tempest*, while the upper stage was certainly the balcony from which Romeo climbs down in Act III of *Romeo and Juliet*.

It can be seen that such a building, simple but adaptable, was not really unsuited to the presentation of plays like Shakespeare's. On the contrary, its simplicity guaranteed the minimum of distraction, while its shape and construction must have produced a sense of involvement on the part of the audience that modern producers would envy.

Other Resources of the Elizabethan Theatre

Although there were few attempts at scenery in the public theatre (painted backcloths were occasionally used in court performances), Shakespeare and his fellow playwrights were able to make use of a fair variety of 'properties', lists of such articles have survived: they include beds, tables, thrones, and also trees, walls, a gallows, a Trojan horse and a 'Mouth of Hell'; in a list of properties belonging to the manager, Philip Henslowe, the curious item 'two mossy banks' appears. Possibly one of them was used for the

> bank whereon the wild thyme blows,
> Where oxlips and the nodding violet grows

in *A Midsummer Night's Dream* (Act II, Scene i). Once again, imagination must have been required of the audience.

Costumes were the one aspect of stage production in which

trouble and expense were hardly ever spared to obtain a magnificent effect. Only occasionally did they attempt any historical accuracy (almost all Elizabethan productions were what we should call 'modern-dress' ones), but they were appropriate to the characters who wore them: kings were seen to be kings and beggars were similarly unmistakable. It is an odd fact that there was usually no attempt at illusion in the costuming: if a costume looked fine and rich it probably was. Indeed, some of the costumes were almost unbelievably expensive. Henslowe lent his company £19 to buy a cloak, and the Alleyn brothers, well-known actors, gave £20 for a 'black velvet cloak, with sleeves embroidered all with silver and gold, lined with black satin striped with gold'.

With the one exception of the costumes, the 'machinery' of the playhouse was economical and uncomplicated rather than crude and rough, as we can see from this second and more leisurely look at it. This meant that playwrights were stimulated to produce the imaginative effects that they wanted from the language that they used. In the case of a really great writer like Shakespeare, when he had learned his trade in the theatre as an actor, it seems that he received quite enough assistance of a mechanical and structural kind without having irksome restrictions and conventions imposed on him; it is interesting to try to guess what he would have done with the highly complex apparatus of a modern television studio. We can see when we look back to his time that he used his instrument, the Elizabethan theatre, to the full, but placed his ultimate reliance on the communication between his imagination and that of his audience through the medium of words. It is, above all, his rich and wonderful use of language that must have made play-going at that time a memorable experience for people of widely different kinds. Fortunately, the deep satisfaction of appreciating and enjoying Shakespeare's work can be ours also, if we are willing to overcome the language difficulty produced by the passing of time.

Shakespeare: A Timeline

Very little indeed is known about Shakespeare's private life; the facts included here are almost the only indisputable ones. The dates of Shakespeare's plays are those on which they were first produced.

1558 Queen Elizabeth crowned.

1561 Francis Bacon born.

1564 Christopher Marlowe born.   William Shakespeare born, April 23rd, baptized April 26th.

1566   Shakespeare's brother, Gilbert, born.

1567 Mary, Queen of Scots, deposed.
      James VI (later James I of England) crowned King of Scotland.

1572 Ben Jonson born.
      Lord Leicester's Company (of players) licensed; later called Lord Strange's, then the Lord Chamberlain's and finally (under James) the King's Men.

1573 John Donne born.

1574 The Common Council of London directs that all plays and playhouses in London must be licensed.

1576 James Burbage builds the first public playhouse, The Theatre, at Shoreditch, outside the walls of the City.

1577 Francis Drake begins his voyage round the world (completed 1580).
      Holinshed's Chronicles of England, Scotland and Ireland published (which

Shakespeare later used extensively).

1582		Shakespeare married to Anne Hathaway.
1583	The Queen's Company founded by royal warrant.	Shakespeare's daughter, Susanna, born.
1585		Shakespeare's twins, Hamnet and Judith, born.
1586	Sir Philip Sidney, the Elizabethan ideal 'Christian knight', poet, patron, soldier, killed at Zutphen in the Low Countries.	
1587	Mary, Queen of Scots, beheaded. Marlowe's *Tamburlaine (Part I)* first staged.	
1588	Defeat of the Spanish Armada. Marlowe's *Tamburlaine (Part II)* first staged.	
1589	Marlowe's *Jew of Malta* and Kyd's *Spanish Tragedy* (a 'revenge tragedy' and one of the most popular plays of Elizabethan times).	
1590	Spenser's *Faerie Queene* (Books I–III) published.	
1592	Marlowe's *Doctor Faustus* and *Edward II* first staged. Witchcraft trials in Scotland. Robert Greene, a rival playwright, refers to Shakespeare as 'an upstart crow' and 'the only Shake-scene in a country'.	*Titus Andronicus* *Henry VI, Parts I, II and III* *Richard III*
1593	London theatres closed by the plague. Christopher Marlowe killed in a Deptford tavern.	*Two Gentlemen of Verona* *Comedy of Errors* *The Taming of the Shrew* *Love's Labour's Lost*
1594	Shakespeare's company becomes The Lord Chamberlain's Men.	*Romeo and Juliet*

1595	Raleigh's first expedition to Guiana. Last expedition of Drake and Hawkins (both died).	*Richard II* *A Midsummer Night's Dream*
1596	Spenser's *Faerie Queene* (Books IV–VI) published. James Burbage buys rooms at Blackfriars and begins to convert them into a theatre.	*King John* *The Merchant of Venice* Shakespeare's son Hamnet dies. Shakespeare's father is granted a coat of arms.
1597	James Burbage dies, his son Richard, a famous actor, turns the Blackfriars Theatre into a private playhouse.	*Henry IV (Part I)* Shakespeare buys and redecorates New Place at Stratford.
1598	Death of Philip II of Spain	*Henry IV (Part II)* *Much Ado About Nothing*
1599	Death of Edmund Spenser. The Globe Theatre completed at Bankside by Richard and Cuthbert Burbage.	*Henry V* *Julius Caesar* *As You Like It*
1600	Fortune Theatre built at Cripplegate. East India Company founded for the extension of English trade and influence in the East. The Children of the Chapel begin to use the hall at Blackfriars.	*Merry Wives of Windsor* *Troilus and Cressida*
1601		*Hamlet*
1602	Sir Thomas Bodley's library opened at Oxford.	*Twelfth Night*
1603	Death of Queen Elizabeth. James I comes to the throne. Shakespeare's company becomes The King's Men. Raleigh tried, condemned and sent to the Tower	
1604	Treaty of peace with Spain	*Measure for Measure* *Othello* *All's Well that Ends Well*
1605	The Gunpowder Plot: an attempt by a group of Catholics to blow up the Houses of Parliament.	

1606	Guy Fawkes and other plotters executed.	*Macbeth* *King Lear*
1607	Virginia, in America, colonized. A great frost in England.	*Antony and Cleopatra* *Timon of Athens* *Coriolanus* Shakespeare's daughter, Susanna, married to Dr. John Hall.
1608	The company of the Children of the Chapel Royal (who had performed at Blackfriars for ten years) is disbanded. John Milton born. Notorious pirates executed in London.	Richard Burbage leases the Blackfriars Theatre to six of his fellow actors, including Shakespeare. *Pericles, Prince of Tyre*
1609		Shakespeare's Sonnets published.
1610	A great drought in England	*Cymbeline*
1611	Chapman completes his great translation of the *Iliad*, the story of Troy. Authorized Version of the Bible published.	*A Winter's Tale* *The Tempest*
1612	Webster's *The White Devil* first staged.	Shakespeare's brother, Gilbert, dies.
1613	Globe theatre burnt down during a performance of *Henry VIII* (the firing of small cannon set fire to the thatched roof). Webster's *Duchess of Malfi* first staged.	*Henry VIII* *Two Noble Kinsmen* Shakespeare buys a house at Blackfriars.
1614	Globe Theatre rebuilt in 'far finer manner than before'.	
1616	Ben Jonson publishes his plays in one volume. Raleigh released from the Tower in order to prepare an expedition to the gold mines of Guiana.	Shakespeare's daughter, Judith, marries Thomas Quiney. Death of Shakespeare on his birthday, April 23rd.
1618	Raleigh returns to England and is executed on the charge for which he was imprisoned in 1603.	
1623	Publication of the Folio edition of Shakespeare's plays	Death of Anne Shakespeare (née Hathaway).

Life & Times

William Shakespeare the Playwright

There exists a curious paradox when it comes to the life of William Shakespeare. He easily has more words written about him than any other famous English writer, yet we know the least about him. This inevitably means that most of what is written about him is either fabrication or speculation. The reason why so little is known about Shakespeare is that he wasn't a novelist or a historian or a man of letters. He was a playwright, and playwrights were considered fairly low on the social pecking order in Elizabethan society. Writing plays was about providing entertainment for the masses – the great unwashed. It was the equivalent to being a journalist for a tabloid newspaper.

In fact, we only know of Shakespeare's work because two of his friends had the foresight to collect his plays together following his death and have them printed. The only reason they did so was apparently because they rated his talent and thought it would be a shame if his words were lost.

Consequently his body of work has ever since been assessed and reassessed as the greatest contribution to English literature. That is despite the fact that we know that different printers took it upon themselves to heavily edit the material they worked from. We also know that Elizabethan plays were worked and reworked frequently, so that they evolved over time until they were honed to perfection, which means that many different hands played their part in the active writing process. It would therefore be fair to say that any play attributed to Shakespeare is unlikely to contain a great deal of original input. Even the plots were based on well known historical events, so it would be hard to know what fragments of any Shakespeare play came from that single mind.

One might draw a comparison with the Christian bible, which remains such a compelling read because it came from the collaboration of many contributors and translators over centuries, who each adjusted the stories until they could no longer be improved. As virtually nothing is known of Shakespeare's life and even less about his method of working, we shall never know the truth about his plays. They certainly contain some very elegant phrasing, clever plot devices and plenty of words never before seen in print, but as to whether Shakespeare invented them from a unique imagination or whether he simply took them from others around him is anyone's guess.

The best bet seems to be that Shakespeare probably took the lead role in devising the original drafts of the plays, but was open to collaboration from any source when it came to developing them into workable scripts for effective performances. He would have had to work closely with his fellow actors in rehearsals, thereby finding out where to edit, abridge, alter, reword and so on.

In turn, similar adjustments would have occurred in his absence, so that definitive versions of his plays never really existed. In effect Shakespeare was only responsible for providing the framework of plays, upon which others took liberties over time. This wasn't helped by the fact that the English language itself was not definitive at that time either. The consequence was that people took it upon themselves to spell words however they pleased or to completely change words and phrasing to suit their own preferences.

It is easy to see then, that Shakespeare's plays were always going to have lives of their own, mutating and distorting in detail like Chinese whispers. The culture of creative preservation was simply not established in Elizabethan England. Creative ownership of Shakespeare's plays was lost to him as soon as he released them into the consciousness of others. They saw nothing wrong with taking his ideas and running with them, because no one had ever suggested that one shouldn't, and Shakespeare probably regarded his work in the same way. His plays weren't sacrosanct works of art, they were templates for theatre folk to make their livings from, so they had every right to mould them into productions that drew in the crowds as effectively as possible. Shakespeare was like the helmsman of a sailing ship, steering the vessel but wholly reliant on the team work of his crew to arrive at the desired destination.

It seems that Shakespeare certainly had a natural gift, but the genius of his plays may be attributable to the collective efforts of Shakespeare and others. It is a rather satisfying notion to think that *his* plays might actually be the creative outpourings of the Elizabethan milieu in which Shakespeare immersed himself. That makes them important social documents as well as seminal works of the English language.

Money in Shakespeare's Day

It is extremely difficult, if not impossible, to relate the value of money in our time to its value in another age and to compare prices of commodities today and in the past. Many items *are* simply not comparable on grounds of quality or serviceability.

There was a bewildering variety of coins in use in Elizabethan England. As nearly all English and European coins were gold or silver, they had intrinsic value apart from their official value. This meant that foreign coins circulated freely in England and were officially recognized, for example the French crown (écu) worth about 30p (72 cents), and the Spanish ducat worth about 33p (79 cents). The following table shows some of the coins mentioned by Shakespeare and their relation to one another.

GOLD	British	American	SILVER	British	American
sovereign (heavy type)	£1.50	$3.60	shilling	10p	24c
sovereign (light type)	66p–£1	$1.58–$2.40	groat	1.5p	4c
angel					
royal	33p–50p	79c–$1.20			
noble	50p	$1.20			
crown	25p	60c			

A comparison of the following prices in Shakespeare's time with the prices of the same items today will give some idea of the change in the value of money.

ITEM	PRICE British	American	ITEM	PRICE British	American
beef, per lb.	0.5p	1c	cherries (lb.)	1p	2c
mutton, leg	7.5p	18c	7 oranges	1p	2c
rabbit	3.5p	9c	1 lemon	1p	2c
chicken	3p	8c	cream (quart)	2.5p	6c
potatoes (lb)	10p	24c	sugar (lb.)	£1	$2.40
carrots (bunch)	1p	2c	sack (wine) (gallon)	14p	34c
8 artichokes	4p	9c	tobacco (oz.)	25p	60c
1 cucumber	1p	2c	biscuits (lb.)	12.5p	30c

INTRODUCTION

Julius Caesar is a study of division in the state and in the self: a divided city, a divided hero, a divided response from the reader to the key characters and central action of the play – is Caesar demigod or braggart, is Brutus noble or foolish, what is the morality of the pre-emptive strike, the ethics of political assassination? The civil war, which is the basic subject-matter, permeates every aspect of the play.

In the opening scene is a joke that touches the core of the play's meaning. Flavius, supporter of the side in the civil war just vanquished by Caesar, indignantly asks a workman why he is so inappropriately making holiday by leading his men through the streets. The man, a cobbler, pertly replies: 'Truly, sir, to wear out their shoes to get myself into more work', before supplying the 'real' reason – to celebrate Caesar's triumph. The jocosely divided motives of the cobbler are a comic anticipation of the tragic dilemma of the central character. In addition, the answer opens a door upon the key question of the play: the nature of politics and the motives of those who participate therein. Cassius and Brutus are also leading men about the streets in a conspiracy that will end in Caesar's assassination. Are they doing it from self-interest or higher motives?

Cassius is easy to understand because there is no division in him. He is simply envy masquerading as principle, resentful of Caesar because he himself would be Caesar, an up-market version of the self-interested cobbler, leading his men for his own advantage. Antony and Octavius are also all too easily comprehensible as they coldbloodedly carve up the spoils, cynically bartering the lives of their closest kinsmen, each concerned only with clawing as much power for himself as he can. These are the single-minded people in the play who so uncomplicatedly, unagonisingly know what they want.

Brutus, by contrast, solicits our interest because he is double, the divided man par excellence, cruelly torn between competing obligations – affection for Caesar (his 'best lover') and concern for the good of Rome, split between friendship and patriotism. The civil war in Rome is also waged within Brutus himself, as he reluctantly consents to Caesar's death (Cassius is avid for it); if only, he laments, they could destroy Caesarism without harming Caesar himself. Unlike Cassius, Brutus acts from principle; he does what he thinks is right and it turns out to be disastrously wrong. The republican era is over – 'our day is gone', says Titinius at Philippi, but this is true from the outset: Rome is destined for Caesarism – the only thing doubtful is the identity of the Caesar. This is made ironically manifest in the acclamation of the crowd at the close of Brutus's speech justifying his enforced killing of Caesar: 'let him be Caesar'. The people want to reward him for what he has done by making him the very thing he loathes most of all – he is to become the man he killed; he has killed for nothing.

Brutus is yesterday's man; the killing of Caesar is revealed as a political blunder of the first magnitude. The man Caesar, arrogant, deaf, so easily swayed, is dead, but the spirit of Caesar lives on. Brutus tries to resist history, stand up against Caesarism, and is ruthlessly swept aside. Hence the justification of the play's title, named for a character who departs the scene with two acts still to go. Caesar, dead, continues to control the action:

> O Julius Caesar, thou art mighty yet!
> Thy spirit walks abroad, and turns our swords
> In our own proper entrails [5.3.94–96].

Brutus has blundered and he pays the ultimate forfeit.

But, Dante notwithstanding, Shakespeare presents him as a good if mistaken man. At the beginning, Cassius, speaking in soliloquy, calls him noble and tells us that, were the positions reversed, i.e. if Caesar favoured Cassius as he so clearly does Brutus, then he, Cassius, would never have been tempted to join the conspiracy. This candid admission confirms the envious, malcontent character of Cassius, while simultaneously vindicating the integrity of Brutus; whatever else, he did not become a conspirator for the cobbler's reason, private gain. Casca, too, tells us that the conspiracy needs Brutus as the one irreproachable man, respected by everyone, whose participation will indemnify the assassins and present their action in the most favourable light. And, at the close, the victory won and the need for propaganda, i.e. lies, removed, Antony, Brutus's foremost enemy, says the same thing over the corpse:

> This was the noblest Roman of them all.
> All the conspirators save only he
> Did what they did in envy of great Caesar. [5.5.68–70]

Dante consigns him to the lowest pit in hell; Shakespeare, it is clear, holds a very different view.

LIST OF CHARACTERS

Julius Caesar

Octavius Caesar
Marcus Antonius } Triumvirs after the
M. Aemil. Lepidus death of Julius Caesar

Cicero
Publius } senators
Popilius Lena

Marcus Brutus
Cassius
Casca
Trebonius
Ligarius } conspirators against Julius Caesar
Decius Brutus
Metellus Cimber
Cinna

Flavius And Marullus   tribunes

Artemidorus   a sophist of Cnidos

A Soothsayer

Cinna   a poet

Another Poet

Lucilius
Titinius
Messala } friends to Brutus and Cassius
Young Cato
Volumnius

Varro
Clitus
Claudius } servants to Brutus
Strato
Lucius
Dardanius

Pindarus	servant to Cassius
Calphurnia	wife to Caesar
Portia	wife to Brutus

Senators, *Citizens*, *Guards*, and *Attendants* etc.

The scene: Rome; Near Sardis; Near Philippi.

ACT ONE
Scene I

Rome. A street.

[Enter FLAVIUS, MARULLUS, *and certain Commoners over the stage.]*

Flavius
    Hence! home, you idle creatures, get you home.
    Is this a holiday? What! know you not,
    Being mechanical, you ought not walk
    Upon a labouring day without the sign
    Of your profession? Speak, what trade art thou?   5

1 Citizen
    Why, sir, a carpenter.

Marullus
    Where is thy leather apron and thy rule?
    What dost thou with thy best apparel on?
    You, sir, what trade are you?

2 Citizen
    Truly, sir, in respect of a fine workman, I am but, as you   10
    would say, a cobbler.

Marullus
    But what trade art thou? Answer me directly.

2 Citizen
    A trade, sir, that I hope I may use with a safe conscience,
    which is indeed, sir, a mender of bad soles.

Marullus
    What trade, thou knave? Thou naughty knave, what   15
    trade?

2 Citizen
    Nay, I beseech you, sir, be not out with me; yet, if you
    be out, sir, I can mend you.

Marullus
    What mean'st thou by that? Mend me, thou saucy fellow!

2 Citizen

20   Why, sir, cobble you.

Flavius

Thou art a cobbler, art thou?

2 Citizen

Truly, sir, all that I live by is with the awl. I meddle with
no tradesman's matters nor women's matters, but with
awl. I am indeed, sir, a surgeon to old shoes. When they

25   are in great danger, I re-cover them. As proper men
as ever trod upon neat's leather have gone upon my
handiwork.

Flavius

But wherefore art not in thy shop today?

Why dost thou lead these men about the streets?

2 Citizen

30   Truly, sir, to wear out their shoes, to get myself into
more work. But indeed, sir, we make holiday to see
Caesar, and to rejoice in his triumph.

Marullus

Wherefore rejoice? What conquest brings he home?

What tributaries follow him to Rome,

35   To grace in captive bonds his chariot wheels?
You blocks, you stones, you worse than senseless
        things!
O you hard hearts, you cruel men of Rome,
Knew you not Pompey? Many a time and oft
Have you climb'd up to walls and battlements,

40   To tow'rs and windows, yea, to chimney-tops,
Your infants in your arms, and there have sat
The livelong day, with patient expectation,
To see great Pompey pass the streets of Rome.
And when you saw his chariot but appear,

45   Have you not made an universal shout,
That Tiber trembled underneath her banks,
To hear the replication of your sounds
Made in her concave shores?
And do you now put on your best attire?

And do you now cull out a holiday? 50
And do you now strew flowers in his way
That comes in triumph over Pompey's blood?
Be gone!
Run to your houses, fall upon your knees,
Pray to the gods to intermit the plague 55
That needs must light on this ingratitude.

Flavius

Go, go, good countrymen, and for this fault
Assemble all the poor men of your sort;
Draw them to Tiber banks, and weep your tears
Into the channel, till the lowest stream 60
Do kiss the most exalted shores of all.

[Exeunt all the Commoners.]

See whe'r their basest metal be not mov'd;
They vanish tongue-tied in their guiltiness.
Go you down that way towards the Capitol;
This way will I. Disrobe the images 65
If you do find them deck'd with ceremonies.

Marullus

May we do so?
You know it is the feast of Lupercal.

Flavius

It is no matter; let no images
Be hung with Caesar's trophies. I'll about, 70
And drive away the vulgar from the streets;
So do you too, where you perceive them thick.
These growing feathers pluck'd from Caesar's wing
Will make him fly an ordinary pitch,
Who else would soar above the view of men, 75
And keep us all in servile fearfulness.

[Exeunt.]

Scene II

Rome. A public place.

[Music. Enter CAESAR*;* ANTONY, *for the course;*
CALPHURNIA, PORTIA, DECIUS, CICERO, BRUTUS,
CASSIUS, *and* CASCA*; a great crowd following, among
them a Soothsayer; after them,* MARULLUS *and* FLAVIUS.*]*

Caesar
    Calphurnia.
Casca
                    Peace, ho! Caesar speaks.

[Music ceases.]

Caesar
    Calphurnia.
Calphurnia
    Here, my lord.
Caesar
                    Stand you directly in Antonius' way
    When he doth run his course. Antonius!
Antony
5   Caesar, my lord.
Caesar
    Forget not in your speed, Antonius,
    To touch Calphurnia; for our elders say,
    The barren, touched in this holy chase,
    Shake off their sterile curse.
Antony
                            I shall remember.
10 When Caesar says 'Do this', it is perform'd.
Caesar
    Set on, and leave no ceremony out.

[Music.]

Soothsayer
    Caesar!

Caesar
   Ha! Who calls?
Casca
   Bid every noise be still. Peace yet again.

                    [Music ceases.]

Caesar
   Who is it in the press that calls on me?   15
   I hear a tongue, shriller than all the music,
   Cry 'Caesar!' Speak. Caesar is turn'd to hear.
Soothsayer
   Beware the ides of March.
Caesar
                         What man is that?
Brutus
   A soothsayer bids you beware the ides of March.
Caesar
   Set him before me; let me see his face.   20
Cassius
   Fellow, come from the throng; look upon Caesar.
Caesar
   What say'st thou to me now? Speak once again.
Soothsayer
   Beware the ides of March.
Caesar
   He is a dreamer; let us leave him.
   Pass.

       [Sennet. Exeunt all but BRUTUS and CASSIUS.]

Cassius
                 Will you go see the order of the course?   25
Brutus
   Not I.
Cassius
   I pray you do.
Brutus
   I am not gamesome: I do lack some part

Of that quick spirit that is in Antony.
30 Let me not hinder, Cassius, your desires;
I'll leave you.

Cassius

Brutus, I do observe you now of late;
I have not from your eyes that gentleness
And show of love as I was wont to have.
35 You bear too stubborn and too strange a hand
Over your friend that loves you.

Brutus

Cassius,
Be not deceiv'd. If I have veil'd my look,
I turn the trouble of my countenance
Merely upon myself. Vexed I am
40 Of late with passions of some difference,
Conceptions only proper to myself,
Which give some soil, perhaps, to my behaviours;
But let not therefore my good friends be griev'd –
Among which number, Cassius, be you one –
45 Nor construe any further my neglect
Than that poor Brutus, with himself at war,
Forgets the shows of love to other men.

Cassius

Then, Brutus, I have much mistook your passion,
By means whereof this breast of mine hath buried
50 Thoughts of great value, worthy cogitations.
Tell me, good Brutus, can you see your face?

Brutus

No, Cassius; for the eye sees not itself
But by reflection, by some other things.

Cassius

'Tis just;
55 And it is very much lamented, Brutus,
That you have no such mirrors as will turn
Your hidden worthiness into your eye,
That you might see your shadow. I have heard,
Where many of the best respect in Rome –

Except immortal Caesar – speaking of Brutus,   60
And groaning underneath this age's yoke,
Have wish'd that noble Brutus had his eyes.

Brutus

Into what dangers would you lead me, Cassius,
That you would have me seek into myself
For that which is not in me?   65

Cassius

Therefore, good Brutus, be prepar'd to hear;
And since you know you cannot see yourself
So well as by reflection, I, your glass,
Will modestly discover to yourself
That of yourself which you yet know not of.   70
And be not jealous on me, gentle Brutus:
Were I a common laughter, or did use
To stale with ordinary oaths my love
To every new protester; if you know
That I do fawn on men and hug them hard,   75
And after scandal them; or if you know
That I profess myself in banqueting
To all the rout, then hold me dangerous.

[Flourish and shout.]

Brutus

What means this shouting? I do fear the people
Choose Caesar for their king.

Cassius

                              Ay, do you fear it?   80
Then must I think you would not have it so.

Brutus

I would not, Cassius; yet I love him well.
But wherefore do you hold me here so long?
What is it that you would impart to me?
If it be aught toward the general good,   85
Set honour in one eye and death i' th' other,
And I will look on both indifferently;
For let the gods so speed me as I love

The name of honour more than I fear death.

Cassius

90   I know that virtue to be in you, Brutus,
As well as I do know your outward favour.
Well, honour is the subject of my story.
I cannot tell what you and other men
Think of this life; but, for my single self,

95   I had as lief not be as live to be
In awe of such a thing as I myself.
I was born free as Caesar; so were you.
We both have fed as well, and we can both
Endure the winter's cold as well as he.

100   For once, upon a raw and gusty day,
The troubled Tiber chafing with her shores,
Caesar said to me 'Dar'st thou, Cassius, now
Leap in with me into this angry flood,
And swim to yonder point?' Upon the word,

105   Accoutred as I was, I plunged in
And bade him follow. So indeed he did.
The torrent roar'd, and we did buffet it
With lusty sinews, throwing it aside
And stemming it with hearts of controversy;

110   But ere we could arrive the point propos'd,
Caesar cried 'Help me, Cassius, or I sink!'
I, as AEneas, our great ancestor,
Did from the flames of Troy upon his shoulder
The old Anchises bear, so from the waves of Tiber

115   Did I the tired Caesar. And this man
Is now become a god; and Cassius is
A wretched creature, and must bend his body
If Caesar carelessly but nod on him.
He had a fever when he was in Spain,

120   And when the fit was on him I did mark
How he did shake. 'Tis true, this god did shake.
His coward lips did from their colour fly,
And that same eye, whose bend doth awe the world,
Did lose his lustre. I did hear him groan.

Ay, and that tongue of his, that bade the Romans   125
Mark him, and write his speeches in their books,
Alas! it cried 'Give me some drink, Titinius'
As a sick girl. Ye gods! it doth amaze me
A man of such a feeble temper should
So get the start of the majestic world,   130
And bear the palm alone. *[Shout. Flourish.]*

Brutus

Another general shout!
I do believe that these applauses are
For some new honours that are heap'd on Caesar.

Cassius

Why, man, he doth bestride the narrow world   135
Like a Colossus, and we petty men
Walk under his huge legs, and peep about
To find ourselves dishonourable graves.
Men at some time are masters of their fates:
The fault, dear Brutus, is not in our stars,   140
But in ourselves, that we are underlings.
'Brutus' and 'Caesar'. What should be in that 'Caesar'?
Why should that name be sounded more than yours?
Write them together: yours is as fair a name.
Sound them: it doth become the mouth as well.   145
Weigh them: it as heavy. Conjure with 'em:
'Brutus' will start a spirit as soon as 'Caesar'.
Now, in the names of all the gods at once,
Upon what meat doth this our Caesar feed,
That he is grown so great? Age, thou art sham'd!   150
Rome, thou has lost the breed of noble bloods!
When went there by an age, since the great flood,
But it was fam'd with more than with one man?
When could they say, till now, that talk'd of Rome,
That her wide walls encompass'd but one man?   155
Now is it Rome indeed, and room enough,
When there is in it but one only man.
O! you and I have heard our fathers say
There was a Brutus once that would have brook'd

160   Th' eternal devil to keep his state in Rome
        As easily as a king.

Brutus
        That you do love me, I am nothing jealous;
        What you would work me to, I have some aim;
        How I have thought of this, and of these times,
165   I shall recount hereafter. For this present,
        I would not, so with love I might entreat you,
        Be any further mov'd. What you have said
        I will consider; what you have to say
        I will with patience hear; and find a time
170   Both meet to hear and answer such high things.
        Till then, my noble friend, chew upon this:
        Brutus had rather be a villager
        Than to repute himself a son of Rome
        Under these hard conditions as this time
175   Is like to lay upon us.

Cassius
        I am glad that my weak words
        Have struck but thus much show of fire from Brutus.

                [Re-enter CAESAR and his Train.]

Brutus
        The games are done, and Caesar is returning.

Cassius
        As they pass by, pluck Casca by the sleeve,
180   And he will, after his sour fashion, tell you
        What hath proceeded worthy note to-day.

Brutus
        I will do so. But, look you, Cassius,
        The angry spot doth glow on Caesar's brow,
        And all the rest look like a children train;
185   Calphurnia's cheek is pale, and Cicero
        Looks with such ferret and such fiery eyes
        As we have seen him in the Capitol,
        Being cross'd in conference by some senators.

Cassius
    Casca will tell us what the matter is.

Caesar
    Antonius! 190

Antony
    Caesar?

Caesar
    Let me have men about me that are fat;
    Sleek-headed men, and such as sleep o' nights.
    Yond Cassius has a lean and hungry look;
    He thinks too much. Such men are dangerous. 195

Antony
    Fear him not, Caesar, he's not dangerous;
    He is a noble Roman, and well given.

Caesar
    Would he were fatter! But I fear him not.
    Yet if my name were liable to fear,
    I do not know the man I should avoid 200
    So soon as that spare Cassius. He reads much,
    He is a great observer, and he looks
    Quite through the deeds of men. He loves no plays,
    As thou dost, Antony; he hears no music.
    Seldom he smiles, and smiles in such a sort 205
    As if he mock'd himself, and scorn'd his spirit
    That could be mov'd to smile at anything.
    Such men as he be never at heart's ease
    Whiles they behold a greater than themselves,
    And therefore are they very dangerous. 210
    I rather tell thee what is to be fear'd
    Than what I fear; for always I am Caesar.
    Come on my right hand, for this ear is deaf,
    And tell me truly what thou think'st of him.

[Sennet. Exeunt CAESAR and his Train.]

Casca
    You pull'd me by the cloak. Would you speak with me? 215

Brutus

Ay, Casca; tell us what hath chanc'd to-day,
That Caesar looks so sad?

Casca

Why, you were with him, were you not?

Brutus

I should not then ask Casca what had chanc'd.

Casca

220 Why, there was a crown offer'd him; and being offer'd
him, he put it by with the back of his hand, thus; and
then the people fell a-shouting.

Brutus

What was the second noise for?

Casca

Why, for that too.

Cassius

225 They shouted thrice; what was the last cry for?

Casca

Why, for that too.

Brutus

Was the crown offer'd him thrice?

Casca

Ay, marry, was't, and he put it by thrice, every time
gentler than other; and at every putting by mine
230 honest neighbours shouted.

Cassius

Who offer'd him the crown?

Casca

Why, Antony.

Brutus

Tell us the manner of it, gentle Casca.

Casca

I can as well be hang'd as tell the manner of it: it was
235 mere foolery; I did not mark it. I saw Mark Antony offer
him a crown – yet 'twas not a crown neither, 'twas one
of these coronets – and, as I told you, he put it by once;
but for all that, to my thinking, he would fain have

had it. Then he offered it to him again; then he put
it by again; but to my thinking, he was very loath to 240
lay his fingers off it. And then he offered it the third
time; he put it the third time by; and still as he refus'd
it, the rabblement hooted, and clapp'd their chopt
hands, and threw up their sweaty night-caps, and
uttered such a deal of stinking breath because Caesar 245
refus'd the crown, that it had almost choked Caesar;
for he swooned and fell down at it. And for mine own
part I durst not laugh, for fear of opening my lips and
receiving the bad air.

Cassius

But soft, I pray you. What, did Caesar swoon? 250

Casca

He fell down in the market-place, and foam'd at mouth,
and was speechless.

Brutus

'Tis very like. He hath the falling sickness.

Cassius

No, Caesar hath it not; but you, and I,
And honest Casca, we have the falling sickness. 255

Casca

I know not what you mean by that, but I am sure
Caesar fell down. If the tag-rag people did not clap him
and hiss him, according as he pleas'd and displeas'd
them, as they use to do the players in the theatre, I am
no true man. 260

Brutus

What said he when he came unto himself?

Casca

Marry, before he fell down, when he perceiv'd the
common herd was glad he refus'd the crown, he
pluckt me ope his doublet, and offer'd them his throat
to cut. An I had been a man of any occupation, if I 265
would not have taken him at a word, I would I might
go to hell among the rogues. And so he fell. When
he came to himself again, he said, if he had done or

270 said anything amiss, he desir'd their worships to think it was his infirmity. Three or four wenches, where I stood, cried 'Alas, good soul!' and forgave him with all their hearts. But there's no heed to be taken of them; if Caesar had stabb'd their mothers, they would have done no less.

Brutus

275 And after that, he came thus sad away?

Casca

Ay.

Cassius

Did Cicero say anything?

Casca

Ay, he spoke Greek.

Cassius

To what effect?

Casca

280 Nay, an I tell you that, I'll ne'er look you i' th' face again. But those that understood him smil'd at one another, and shook their heads; but for mine own part, it was Greek to me. I could tell you more news too: Marullus and Flavius, for pulling scarfs off Caesar's images, are

285 put to silence. Fare you well. There was more foolery yet, if I could remember it.

Cassius

Will you sup with me to-night, Casca?

Casca

No, I am promis'd forth.

Cassius

Will you dine with me to-morrow?

Casca

290 Ay, if I be alive, and your mind hold, and your dinner worth the eating.

Cassius

Good; I will expect you.

Casca

Do so. Farewell, both. *[Exit.]*

Brutus

 What a blunt fellow is this grown to be!

 He was quick mettle when he went to school.   295

Cassius

 So is he now, in execution

 Of any bold or noble enterprise,

 However he puts on this tardy form.

 This rudeness is a sauce to his good wit,

 Which gives men stomach to digest his words   300

 With better appetite.

Brutus

 And so it is. For this time I will leave you.

 To-morrow, if you please to speak with me,

 I will come home to you; or, if you will,

 Come home to me, and I will wait for you.   305

Cassius

 I will do so. Till then, think of the world. *[Exit* BRUTUS.*]*

 Well, Brutus, thou art noble; yet, I see,

 Thy honourable metal may be wrought

 From that it is dispos'd. Therefore it is meet

 That noble minds keep ever with their likes;   310

 For who so firm that cannot be seduc'd?

 Caesar doth bear me hard; but he loves Brutus.

 If I were Brutus now and he were Cassius,

 He should not humour me. I will this night,

 In several hands, in at his windows throw,   315

 As if they came from several citizens,

 Writings, all tending to the great opinion

 That Rome holds of his name; wherein obscurely

 Caesar's ambition shall be glanced at.

 And, after this, let Caesar seat him sure;   320

 For we will shake him, or worse days endure.

[Exit.]

Scene III

Rome. A street.

[Thunder and lightning. Enter, from opposite sides,
CASCA, with his sword drawn, and CICERO.]

Cicero
Good even, Casca. Brought you Caesar home?
Why are you breathless? and why stare you so?
Casca
Are not you mov'd, when all the sway of earth
Shakes like a thing unfirm? O Cicero,
5   I have seen tempests when the scolding winds
Have riv'd the knotty oaks, and I have seen
Th' ambitious ocean swell, and rage, and foam,
To be exalted with the threat'ning clouds;
But never till to-night, never till now,
10   Did I go through a tempest dropping fire.
Either there is a civil strife in heaven,
Or else the world, too saucy with the gods,
Incenses them to send destruction.
Cicero
Why, saw you any thing more wonderful?
Casca
15   A common slave – you know him well by sight –
Held up his left hand, which did flame and burn
Like twenty torches join'd; and yet his hand,
Not sensible of fire, remain'd unscorch'd.
Besides – I ha' not since put up my sword –
20   Against the Capitol I met a lion,
Who glaz'd upon me, and went surly by
Without annoying me; and there were drawn
Upon a heap a hundred ghastly women,
Transformed with their fear, who swore they saw
25   Men, all in fire, walk up and down the streets.
And yesterday the bird of night did sit,
Even at noon-day, upon the market-place,

Hooting and shrieking. When these prodigies
Do so conjointly meet, let not men say
'These are their reasons – they are natural',   30
For I believe they are portentous things
Unto the climate that they point upon.

Cicero

Indeed, it is a strange-disposed time;
But men may construe things after their fashion,
Clean from the purpose of the things themselves.   35
Comes Caesar to the Capitol to-morrow?

Casca

He doth; for he did bid Antonius
Send word to you he would be there to-morrow.

Cicero

Good night, then, Casca; this disturbed sky
Is not to walk in.   40

Casca

        Farewell, Cicero. *[Exit CICERO.]*

        [Enter CASSIUS.]

Cassius

Who's there?

Casca

      A Roman.

Cassius

           Casca, by your voice.

Casca

Your ear is good. Cassius, what night is this!

Cassius

A very pleasing night to honest men.

Casca

Who ever knew the heavens menace so?

Cassius

Those that have known the earth so full of faults.   45
For my part, I have walk'd about the streets,
Submitting me unto the perilous night,
And, thus unbraced, Casca, as you see,

Have bar'd my bosom to the thunder-stone;
50 And when the cross blue lighting seem'd to open
The breast of heaven, I did present myself
Even in the aim and very flash of it.

Casca

But wherefore did you so much tempt the heavens?
It is the part of men to fear and tremble
55 When the most mighty gods by tokens send
Such dreadful heralds to astonish us.

Cassius

You are dull, Casca, and those sparks of life
That should be in a Roman you do want,
Or else you use not. You look pale, and gaze,
60 And put on fear, and cast yourself in wonder,
To see the strange impatience of the heavens;
But if you would consider the true cause –
Why all these fires, why all these gliding ghosts,
Why birds and beasts, from quality and kind;
65 Why old men, fools, and children calculate;
Why all these things change from their ordinance,
Their natures and preformed faculties,
To monstrous quality – why, you shall find
That heaven hath infus'd them with these spirits,
70 To make them instruments of fear and warning
Unto some monstrous state.
Now could I, Casca, name to thee a man
Most like this dreadful night
That thunders, lightens, opens graves, and roars
75 As doth the lion in the Capitol;
A man no mightier than thyself or me
In personal action, yet prodigious grown,
And fearful, as these strange eruptions are.

Casca

'Tis Caesar that you mean, is it not, Cassius?

Cassius

80 Let it be who it is; for Romans now
Have thews and limbs like to their ancestors.

But woe the while! our fathers' minds are dead,
And we are govern'd with our mothers' spirits;
Our yoke and sufferance show us womanish.

Casca

Indeed they say the senators to-morrow   85
Mean to establish Caesar as a king;
And he shall wear his crown by sea and land,
In every place save here in Italy.

Cassius

I know where I will wear this dagger then;
Cassius from bondage will deliver Cassius.   90
Therein, ye gods, you make the weak most strong;
Therein, ye gods, you tyrants do defeat.
Nor stony tower, nor walls of beaten brass,
Nor airless dungeon, nor strong links of iron,
Can be retentive to the strength of spirit;   95
But life, being weary of these worldly bars,
Never lacks power to dismiss itself.
If I know this, know all the world besides,
That part of tyranny that I do bear,
I can shake off at pleasure. *[Thunder still.]*

Casca

                                So can I;   100
So every bondman in his own hand bears
The power to cancel his captivity.

Cassius

And why should Caesar be a tyrant, then?
Poor man! I know he would not be a wolf
But that he sees the Romans are but sheep;   105
He were no lion, were not Romans hinds.
Those that with haste will make a mighty fire
Begin it with weak straws. What trash is Rome,
What rubbish, and what offal, when it serves
For the base matter to illuminate   110
So vile a thing as Caesar! But, O grief,
Where hast thou led me? I perhaps speak this
Before a willing bondman; then I know

My answer must be made. But I am arm'd,
115 And dangers are to me indifferent.
Casca
You speak to Casca, and to such a man
That is no fleering tell-tale. Hold, my hand.
Be factious for redress of all these griefs,
And I will set this foot of mine as far
As who goes farthest.
Cassius
120   There's a bargain made.
Now know you, Casca, I have mov'd already
Some certain of the noblest-minded Romans
To undergo with me an enterprise
Of honourable-dangerous consequence;
125 And I do know by this they stay for me
In Pompey's porch; for now, this fearful night,
There is no stir or walking in the streets,
And the complexion of the element
In favour's like the work we have in hand,
130 Most bloody, fiery, and most terrible.

[Enter CINNA.]

Casca
Stand close awhile, for here comes one in haste.
Cassius
'Tis Cinna, I do know him by his gait;
He is a friend. Cinna, where haste you so?
Cinna
To find out you. Who's that? Metellus Cimber?
Cassius
135 No, it is Casca, one incorporate
To our attempts. Am I not stay'd for, Cinna?
Cinna
I am glad on't. What a fearful night is this!
There's two or three of us have seen strange sights.
Cassius
Am I not stay'd for? Tell me.

Cinna

    Yes, you are. O Cassius, if you could   140
    But win the noble Brutus to our party –

Cassius

    Be you content. Good Cinna, take this paper,
    And look you lay it in the praetor's chair,
    Where Brutus may but find it; and throw this
    In at his window; set this up with wax   145
    Upon old Brutus' statue. All this done,
    Repair to Pompey's porch, where you shall find us.
    Is Decius Brutus and Trebonius there?

Cinna

    All but Metellus Cimber, and he's gone
    To seek you at your house. Well, I will hie,   150
    And so bestow these papers as you bade me.

Cassius

    That done, repair to Pompey's theatre.

[Exit CINNA.]

    Come, Casca, you and I will yet ere day
    See Brutus at his house. Three parts of him
    Is ours already, and the man entire   155
    Upon the next encounter yields him ours.

Casca

    O, he sits high in all the people's hearts;
    And that which would appear offence in us
    His countenance, like richest alchemy,
    Will change to virtue and to worthiness.   160

Cassius

    Him and his worth and our great need of him
    You have right well conceited. Let us go,
    For it is after midnight; and ere day
    We will awake him and be sure of him.

[Exeunt.]

ACT TWO
Scene I

Rome.

[Enter BRUTUS in his orchard.]

Brutus
    What, Lucius, ho!
    I cannot by the progress of the stars
    Give guess how near to day. Lucius, I say!
    I would it were my fault to sleep so soundly.
5   When, Lucius, when? Awake, I say! What, Lucius!

[Enter LUCIUS.]

Lucius
    Call'd you, my lord?
Brutus
    Get me a taper in my study, Lucius;
    When it is lighted, come and call me here.
Lucius
    I will, my lord. *[Exit.]*
Brutus
10   It must be by his death; and for my part,
    I know no personal cause to spurn at him,
    But for the general: he would be crown'd.
    How that might change his nature, there's the
        question.
    It is the bright day that brings forth the adder,
15   And that craves wary walking. Crown him – that!
    And then, I grant, we put a sting in him
    That at his will he may do danger with.
    Th' abuse of greatness is, when it disjoins
    Remorse from power; and to speak truth of Caesar,
20   I have not known when his affections sway'd
    More than his reason. But 'tis a common proof

That lowliness is young ambition's ladder,
Whereto the climber-upward turns his face;
But when he once attains the upmost round,
He then unto the ladder turns his back,   25
Looks in the clouds, scorning the base degrees
By which he did ascend. So Caesar may.
Then, lest he may, prevent. And since the quarrel
Will bear no colour for the thing he is,
Fashion it thus – that what he is, augmented,   30
Would run to these and these extremities;
And therefore think him as a serpent's egg,
Which, hatch'd, would as his kind grow mischievous,
And kill him in the shell.

[Re-enter LUCIUS.]

Lucius

The taper burneth in your closet, sir.   35
Searching the window for a flint, I found
This paper, thus seal'd up; and I am sure
It did not lie there when I went to bed.

[Giving him a letter.]

Brutus

Get you to bed again, it is not day.
Is not to-morrow, boy, the ides of March?   40

Lucius

I know not, sir.

Brutus

Look in the calender, and bring me word.

Lucius

I will, sir. *[Exit.]*

Brutus

The exhalations, whizzing in the air,
Give so much light that I may read by them.   45

[Opens the letter and reads.]

'Brutus, thou sleep'st. Awake, and see thyself.

Shall Rome, etc. Speak, strike, redress!
Brutus, thou sleep'st; awake.'
Such instigations have been often dropp'd
50 Where I have took them up.
'Shall Rome, etc.' Thus must I piece it out:
Shall Rome stand under one man's awe? What, Rome?
My ancestors did from the streets of Rome
The Tarquin drive, when he was call'd a king.
55 'Speak, strike, redress!' Am I entreated
To speak and strike? O Rome, I make thee promise,
If the redress will follow, thou receivest
Thy full petition at the hand of Brutus!

[Re-enter LUCIUS.]

Lucius
Sir, March is wasted fifteen days.

[Knocking within.]

Brutus
60 'Tis good. Go to the gate; somebody knocks.

[Exit LUCIUS.]

Since Cassius first did whet me against Caesar, I have
    not slept.
Between the acting of a dreadful thing
And the first motion, all the interim is
Like a phantasma or a hideous dream.
65 The Genius and the mortal instruments
Are then in council; and the state of man,
Like to a little kingdom, suffers then
The nature of an insurrection.

[Re-enter LUCIUS.]

Lucius
Sir, 'tis your brother Cassius at the door
Who doth desire to see you.
Brutus
70   Is he alone?

Lucius
　　No, sir, there are moe with him.
Brutus
　　Do you know them?
Lucius
　　No, sir; their hats are pluck'd about their ears
　　And half their faces buried in their cloaks,
　　That by no means I may discover them　　　　　75
　　By any mark of favour.
Brutus
　　　　　　　　Let 'em enter.

　　　　　[Exit LUCIUS.]

　　They are the faction. O conspiracy,
　　Sham'st thou to show thy dang'rous brow by night,
　　When evils are most free? O, then by day
　　Where wilt thou find a cavern dark enough　　　80
　　To mask thy monstrous visage? Seek none, conspiracy;
　　Hide it in smiles and affability!
　　For if thou path, thy native semblance on,
　　Not Erebus itself were dim enough
　　To hide thee from prevention.　　　　　　　85

　　　　*[Enter the conspirators, CASSIUS, CASCA, DECIUS,
　　　　　CINNA, METELLUS CIMBER, and TREBONIUS.]*

Cassius
　　I think we are too bold upon your rest.
　　Good morrow, Brutus. Do we trouble you?
Brutus
　　I have been up this hour, awake all night.
　　Know I these men that come along with you?
Cassius
　　Yes, every man of them; and no man here　　　90
　　But honours you; and every one doth wish
　　You had but that opinion of yourself
　　Which every noble Roman bears of you.

This is Trebonius.
Brutus

He is welcome hither.
Cassius

This, Decius Brutus.
Brutus
95   He is welcome too.
Cassius

This, Casca; this, Cinna;
And this, Metellus Cimber.
Brutus

They are all welcome.
What watchful cares do interpose themselves
Betwixt your eyes and night?
Cassius
100   Shall I entreat a word? *[They whisper.]*
Decius

Here lies the east. Doth not the day break here?
Casca

No.
Cinna

O, pardon, sir, it doth; and yon grey lines
That fret the clouds are messengers of day.
Casca
105   You shall confess that you are both deceiv'd.
Here, as I point my sword, the sun arises;
Which is a great way growing on the south,
Weighing the youthful season of the year.
Some two months hence up higher toward the north
110   He first presents his fire; and the high east
Stands as the Capitol, directly here.
Brutus

Give me your hands all over, one by one.
Cassius

And let us swear our resolution.
Brutus

No, not an oath. If not the face of men,

The sufferance of our souls, the time's abuse, 115
If these be motives weak, break off betimes,
And every man hence to his idle bed.
So let high-sighted tyranny range on,
Till each man drop by lottery. But if these,
As I am sure they do, bear fire enough 120
To kindle cowards, and to steel with valour
The melting spirits of women, then, countrymen,
What need we any spur but our own cause
To prick us to redress? What other bond
Than secret Romans that have spoke the word 125
And will not palter? And what other oath
Than honesty to honesty engag'd
That this shall be or we will fall for it?
Swear priests and cowards and men cautelous,
Old feeble carrions and such suffering souls 130
That welcome wrongs; unto bad causes swear
Such creatures as men doubt; but do not stain
The even virtue of our enterprise,
Nor th' insuppressive mettle of our spirits,
To think that or our cause or our performance 135
Did need an oath; when every drop of blood
That every Roman bears, and nobly bears,
Is guilty of a several bastardy,
If he do break the smallest particle
Of any promise that hath pass'd from him. 140

Cassius

But what of Cicero? Shall we sound him?
I think he will stand very strong with us.

Casca

Let us not leave him out.

Cinna

                No, by no means.

Metellus

O, let us have him; for his silver hairs
Will purchase us a good opinion, 145
And buy men's voices to commend our deeds.

It shall be said his judgment rul'd our hands;
Our youths and wildness shall no whit appear,
But all be buried in his gravity.

Brutus

150   O, name him not! Let us not break with him;
For he will never follow any thing
That other men begin.

Cassius

                       Then leave him out.

Casca

Indeed he is not fit.

Decius

Shall no man else be touch'd but only Caesar?

Cassius

155   Decius, well urg'd. I think it is not meet
Mark Antony, so well belov'd of Caesar,
Should outlive Caesar. We shall find of him
A shrewd contriver; and you know his means,
If he improve them, may well stretch so far

160   As to annoy us all; which to prevent,
Let Antony and Caesar fall together.

Brutus

Our course will seem too bloody, Caius Cassius,
To cut the head off and then hack the limbs –
Like wrath in death and envy afterwards;

165   For Antony is but a limb of Caesar.
Let's be sacrificers, but not butchers, Caius.
We all stand up against the spirit of Caesar,
And in the spirit of men there is no blood.
O that we then could come by Caesar's spirit,

170   And not dismember Caesar! But, alas,
Caesar must bleed for it! And, gentle friends,
Let's kill him boldly, but not wrathfully;
Let's carve him as a dish fit for the gods,
Not hew him as a carcase fit for hounds;

175   And let our hearts, as subtle masters do,
Stir up their servants to an act of rage,

And after seem to chide 'em. This shall make
Our purpose necessary, and not envious;
Which so appearing to the common eyes,
We shall be call'd purgers, not murderers.   180
And for Mark Antony, think not of him;
For he can do no more than Caesar's arm
When Caesar's head is off.

Cassius
                Yet I fear him;
For in the engrafted love he bears to Caesar –

Brutus
Alas, good Cassius, do not think of him!   185
If he love Caesar, all that he can do
Is to himself take thought and die for Caesar;
And that were much he should, for he is given
To sports, to wildness, and much company.

Trebonius
There is no fear in him. Let him not die;   190
For he will live, and laugh at this hereafter.

[Clock strikes.]

Brutus
Peace! Count the clock.

Cassius
              The clock hath stricken three.

Trebonius
'Tis time to part.

Cassius
          But it is doubtful yet
Whether Caesar will come forth to-day or no;
For he is superstitious grown of late,   195
Quite from the main opinion he held once
Of fantasy, of dreams, and ceremonies.
It may be these apparent prodigies,
The unaccustom'd terror of this night,
And the persuasion of his augurers,   200
May hold him from the Capitol to-day.

Decius
    Never fear that. If he be so resolv'd,
    I can o'ersway him; for he loves to hear
    That unicorns may be betray'd with trees,
205   And bears with glasses, elephants with holes,
    Lions with toils, and men with flatterers;
    But when I tell him he hates flatterers,
    He says he does, being then most flattered.
    Let me work;
210   For I can give his humour the true bent,
    And I will bring him to the Capitol.
Cassius
    Nay, we will all of us be there to fetch him.
Brutus
    By the eighth hour. Is that the uttermost?
Cinna
    Be that the uttermost, and fail not then.
Metellus
215   Caius Ligarius doth bear Caesar hard,
    Who rated him for speaking well of Pompey.
    I wonder none of you have thought of him.
Brutus
    Now, good Metellus, go along by him.
    He loves me well, and I have given him reasons;
220   Send him but hither, and I'll fashion him.
Cassius
    The morning comes upon's. We'll leave you, Brutus.
    And, friends, disperse yourselves; but all remember
    What you have said, and show yourselves true
        Romans.
Brutus
    Good gentlemen, look fresh and merrily;
225   Let not our looks put on our purposes,
    But bear it as our Roman actors do,
    With untir'd spirits and formal constancy.
    And so good morrow to you every one.

[Exeunt all but BRUTUS.]

Boy! Lucius! Fast asleep? It is no matter;
Enjoy the honey-heavy dew of slumber.   230
Thou hast no figures nor no fantasies
Which busy care draws in the brains of men;
Therefore thou sleep'st so sound.

[Enter PORTIA.]

Portia

Brutus, my lord!

Brutus

Portia, what mean you? Wherefore rise you now?
It is not for your health thus to commit   235
Your weak condition to the raw cold morning.

Portia

Nor for yours neither. Y'have ungently, Brutus,
Stole from my bed; and yesternight at supper
You suddenly arose and walk'd about,
Musing and sighing, with your arms across;   240
And when I ask'd you what the matter was,
You star'd upon me with ungentle looks.
I urg'd you further; then you scratch'd your head
And too impatiently stamp'd with your foot.
Yet I insisted; yet you answer'd not,   245
But with an angry wafture of your hand
Gave sign for me to leave you. So I did,
Fearing to strengthen that impatience
Which seem'd too much enkindled; and withal
Hoping it was but an effect of humour,   250
Which sometimes hath his hour with every man.
It will not let you eat, nor talk, nor sleep;
And, could it work so much upon your shape
As it hath much prevail'd on your condition,
I should not know you Brutus. Dear my lord,   255
Make me acquainted with your cause of grief.

Brutus

I am not well in health, and that is all.

Portia
 Brutus is wise, and, were he not in health,
 He would embrace the means to come by it.

Brutus
260 Why, so I do. Good Portia, go to bed.

Portia
 Is Brutus sick, and is it physical
 To walk unbraced and suck up the humours
 Of the dank morning? What, is Brutus sick,
 And will he steal out of his wholesome bed,
265 To dare the vile contagion of the night,
 And tempt the rheumy and unpurged air
 To add unto his sickness? No, my Brutus;
 You have some sick offence within your mind,
 Which by the right and virtue of my place
270 I ought to know of; and upon my knees
 I charm you, by my once-commended beauty,
 By all your vows of love, and that great vow
 Which did incorporate and make us one,
 That you unfold to me, your self, your half,
275 Why you are heavy – and what men to-night
 Have had resort to you; for here have been
 Some six or seven, who did hide their faces
 Even from darkness.

Brutus
       Kneel not, gentle Portia.

Portia
 I should not need, if you were gentle Brutus.
280 Within the bond of marriage, tell me, Brutus,
 Is it excepted I should know no secrets
 That appertain to you? Am I your self
 But, as it were, in sort or limitation?
 To keep with you at meals, comfort your bed,
285 And talk to you sometimes? Dwell I but in the suburbs
 Of your good pleasure? If it be no more,
 Portia is Brutus' harlot, not his wife.

Brutus

    You are my true and honourable wife,
    As dear to me as are the ruddy drops
    That visit my sad heart.   290

Portia

    If this were true, then should I know this secret.
    I grant I am a woman; but withal
    A woman that Lord Brutus took to wife.
    I grant I am a woman; but withal
    A woman well reputed, Cato's daughter.   295
    Think you I am no stronger than my sex,
    Being so father'd and so husbanded?
    Tell me your counsels, I will not disclose 'em.
    I have made strong proof of my constancy,
    Giving myself a voluntary wound   300
    Here, in the thigh. Can I bear that with patience,
    And not my husband's secrets?

Brutus

                         O ye gods,
    Render me worthy of this noble wife!

             [Knocking within.]

    Hark, hark! one knocks. Portia, go in awhile,
    And by and by thy bosom shall partake   305
    The secrets of my heart.
    All my engagements I will construe to thee,
    All the charactery of my sad brows.
    Leave me with haste. *[Exit PORTIA.]*
                  Lucius, who's that knocks?

       [Enter LUCIUS and LIGARIUS.]

Lucius

    Here is a sick man that would speak with you.   310

Brutus

    Caius Ligarius, that Metellus spake of.
    Boy, stand aside. Caius Ligarius, how?

Ligarius
Vouchsafe good morrow from a feeble tongue.
Brutus
O, what a time have you chose out, brave Caius,
315 To wear a kerchief! Would you were not sick!
Ligarius
I am not sick, if Brutus have in hand
Any exploit worthy the name of honour.
Brutus
Such an exploit have I in hand, Ligarius,
Had you a healthful ear to hear of it.
Ligarius
320 By all the gods that Romans bow before,
I here discard my sickness. *[Pulls off his kerchief]* Soul of
    Rome!
Brave son, deriv'd from honourable loins!
Thou, like an exorcist, hast conjur'd up
My mortified spirit. Now bid me run,
325 And I will strive with things impossible;
Yea, get the better of them. What's to do?
Brutus
A piece of work that will make sick men whole.
Ligarius
But are not some whole that we must make sick?
Brutus
That must we also. What it is, my Caius,
330 I shall unfold to thee, as we are going
To whom it must be done.
Ligarius
                              Set on your foot,
And with a heart new-fir'd I follow you
To do I know not what; but it sufficeth
That Brutus leads me on. *[Thunder.]*
Brutus
                              Follow me, then.

[Exeunt.]

Scene II

Rome. Caesar's house.

[Thunder and lightning. Enter JULIUS CAESAR *in his night-gown.]*

Caesar

Nor heaven nor earth have been at peace to-night.
Thrice hath Calphurnia in her sleep cried out
'Help, ho! They murder Caesar!' Who's within?

[Enter a Servant.]

Servant

My lord?

Caesar

Go bid the priests do present sacrifice,   5
And bring me their opinions of success.

Servant

I will, my lord. *[Exit.]*

[Enter CALPHURNIA.*]*

Calphurnia

At mean you, Caesar? Think you to walk forth?
You shall not stir out of your house to-day.

Caesar

Caesar shall forth; the things that threaten'd me   10
Ne'er look'd but on my back. When they shall see
The face of Caesar, they are vanished.

Calphurnia

Caesar, I never stood on ceremonies,
Yet now they fright me. There is one within,
Besides the things that we have heard and seen,   15
Recounts most horrid sights seen by the watch.
A lioness hath whelped in the streets,
And graves have yawn'd and yielded up their dead;
Fierce fiery warriors fight upon the clouds,
In ranks and squadrons and right form of war,   20

Which drizzled blood upon the Capitol;
The noise of battle hurtled in the air;
Horses did neigh, and dying men did groan,
And ghosts did shriek and squeal about the streets.
25 O Caesar, these things are beyond all use,
And I do fear them!

Caesar

               What can be avoided,
Whose end is purpos'd by the mighty gods?
Yet Caesar shall go forth; for these predictions
Are to the world in general as to Caesar.

Calphurnia

30 When beggars die there are no comets seen:
The heavens themselves blaze forth the death of princes.

Caesar

Cowards die many times before their deaths:
The valiant never taste of death but once.
Of all the wonders that I yet have heard,
35 It seems to me most strange that men should fear,
Seeing that death, a necessary end,
Will come when it will come.

[Re-enter Servant.]

               What say the augurers?

Servant

They would not have you to stir forth to-day.
Plucking the entrails of an offering forth,
40 They could not find a heart within the beast.

Caesar

The gods do this in shame of cowardice.
Caesar should be a beast without a heart,
If he should stay at home to-day for fear.
No, Caesar shall not. Danger knows full well
45 That Caesar is more dangerous than he:
We are two lions litter'd in one day,
And I the elder and more terrible;
And Caesar shall go forth.

Calphurnia

Alas, my lord,
Your wisdom is consum'd in confidence.
Do not go forth to-day. Call it my fear   50
That keeps you in the house, and not your own.
We'll send Mark Antony to the Senate House,
And he shall say you are not well to-day.
Let me, upon my knee, prevail in this.

Caesar

Mark Antony shall say I am not well;   55
And for thy humour I will stay at home.

[Enter DECIUS.]

Here's Decius Brutus, he shall tell them so.

Decius

Caesar, all hail! Good morrow, worthy Caesar.
I come to fetch you to the Senate House.

Caesar

And you are come in very happy time,   60
To bear my greeting to the senators
And tell them that I will not come to-day.
Cannot, is false; and that I dare not, falser;
I will not come to-day. Tell them so, Decius.

Calphurnia

Say he is sick.

Caesar

Shall Caesar send a lie?   65
Have I in conquest stretch'd mine arm so far,
To be afeard to tell greybeards the truth?
Decius, go tell them, Caesar will not come.

Decius

Most mighty Caesar, let me know some cause,
Lest I be laugh'd at when I tell them so.   70

Caesar

The cause is in my will: I will not come.
That is enough to satisfy the Senate.
But for your private satisfaction,

Because I love you, I will let you know:
75 Calphurnia here, my wife, stays me at home.
She dreamt to-night she saw my statua,
Which, like a fountain with an hundred spouts,
Did run pure blood; and many lusty Romans
Came smiling and did bathe their hands in it.
80 And these does she apply for warnings and portents
And evils imminent, and on her knee
Hath begg'd that I will stay at home to-day.

Decius

This dream is all amiss interpreted;
It was a vision fair and fortunate.
85 Your statue spouting blood in many pipes,
In which so many smiling Romans bath'd,
Signifies that from you great Rome shall suck
Reviving blood, and that great men shall press
For tinctures, stains, relics, and cognizance.
90 This by Calphurnia's dream is signified.

Caesar

And this way have you well expounded it.

Decius

I have, when you have heard what I can say –
And know it now: the Senate have concluded
To give this day a crown to mighty Caesar.
95 If you shall send them word you will not come,
Their minds may change. Besides, it were a mock
Apt to be render'd, for some one to say
'Break up the Senate till another time,
When Caesar's wife shall meet with better dreams'.
100 If Caesar hide himself, shall they not whisper
'Lo, Caesar is afraid'?
Pardon me, Caesar; for my dear dear love
To your proceeding bids me tell you this,
And reason to my love is liable.

Caesar

105 How foolish do your fears seem now, Calphurnia!
I am ashamed I did yield to them.

Give me my robe, for I will go.

    [Enter BRUTUS, LIGARIUS, METELLUS, CASCA,
        TREBONIUS, CINNA, *and* PUBLIUS.*]*

And look where Publius is come to fetch me.
Publius
    Good morrow, Caesar.
Caesar
                Welcome, Publius.
What, Brutus, are you stirr'd so early too?   110
Good morrow, Casca. Caius Ligarius,
Caesar was ne'er so much your enemy
As that same ague which hath made you lean.
What is't o'clock?
Brutus
            Caesar, 'tis strucken eight.
Caesar
    I thank you for your pains and courtesy.   115

          [Enter ANTONY.*]*

See! Antony, that revels long o' nights,
Is notwithstanding up. Good morrow, Antony.
Antony
    So to most noble Caesar.
Caesar
              Bid them prepare within.
I am to blame to be thus waited for.
Now, Cinna. Now, Metellus. What, Trebonius!
I have an hour's talk in store for you.   120
Remember that you call on me to-day;
Be near me, that I may remember you.
Trebonius
    Caesar, I will. *[Aside]* And so near will I be,
That your best friends shall wish I had been further.

Caesar
125   Good friends, go in and taste some wine with me;
      And we, like friends, will straightway go together.

Brutus
      [Aside] That every like is not the same, O Caesar,
      The heart of Brutus earns to think upon!

[Exeunt.]

Scene III

Rome. A street near the Capitol.

[Enter ARTEMIDORUS reading a paper.]

Artemidorus

'Caesar, beware of Brutus; take heed of Cassius; come
not near Casca; have an eye to Cinna; trust not
Trebonius; mark well Metellus Cimber; Decius Brutus
loves thee not; thou hast wrong'd Caius Ligarius.
There is but one mind in all these men, and it is bent   5
against Caesar. If thou beest not immortal, look about
you. Security gives way to conspiracy. The mighty gods
defend thee!

       Thy lover,

          ARTEMIDORUS.'

Here will I stand till Caesar pass along,
And as a suitor will I give him this.   10
My heart laments that virtue cannot live
Out of the teeth of emulation.
If thou read this, O, Caesar, thou mayest live;
If not, the fates with traitors do contrive.

[Exit.]

Scene IV

Rome. Before the house of Brutus.

[Enter PORTIA and LUCIUS.]

Portia
I prithee, boy, run to the Senate House.
Stay not to answer me, but get thee gone.
Why dost thou stay?

Lucius
                To know my errand, madam.

Portia
I would have had thee there and here again,
5 Ere I can tell thee what thou shouldst do there.
[Aside] O constancy, be strong upon my side!
Set a huge mountain 'tween my heart and tongue!
I have a man's mind, but a woman's might.
How hard it is for women to keep counsel! –
Art thou here yet?

Lucius
10   Madam, what should I do?
Run to the Capitol, and nothing else?
And so return to you, and nothing else?

Portia
Yes, bring me word, boy, if thy lord look well,
For he went sickly forth; and take good note
15 What Caesar doth, what suitors press to him.
Hark, boy! What noise is that?

Lucius
I hear none, madam.

Portia
             Prithee listen well.
I heard a bustling rumour, like a fray,
And the wind brings it from the Capitol.

Lucius
Sooth, madam, I hear nothing.

[Enter the Soothsayer.]

Portia

                          Come hither, fellow.   20
Which way hast thou been?

Soothsayer

                      At mine own house, good lady.

Portia

What is't o'clock?

Soothsayer

                   About the ninth hour, lady.

Portia

Is Caesar yet gone to the Capitol?

Soothsayer

Madam, not yet. I go to take my stand,
To see him pass on to the Capitol.   25

Portia

Thou hast some suit to Caesar, hast thou not?

Soothsayer

That I have, lady. If it will please Caesar
To be so good to Caesar as to hear me,
I shall beseech him to befriend himself.

Portia

Why, know'st thou any harm's intended towards him?   30

Soothsayer

None that I know will be, much that I fear may
    chance.
Good morrow to you. Here the street is narrow;
The throng that follows Caesar at the heels,
Of senators, of praetors, common suitors,
Will crowd a feeble man almost to death.   35
I'll get me to a place more void, and there
Speak to great Caesar as he comes along.

[Exit.]

Portia

I must go in. *[Aside]* Ay me, how weak a thing
The heart of woman is! O Brutus,

40   The heavens speed thee in thine enterprise!
Sure the boy heard me. – Brutus hath a suit
That Caesar will not grant. – O, I grow faint. –
Run, Lucius, and commend me to my lord;
Say I am merry. Come to me again,
45   And bring me word what he doth say to thee.

[Exeunt severally.]

ACT THREE
Scene I

Rome. A street before the Capitol.

[Flourish. Enter CAESAR, BRUTUS, CASSIUS, CASCA,
DECIUS, METELLUS, TREBONIUS, CINNA, ANTONY,
LEPIDUS, ARTEMIDORUS, POPILIUS, PUBLIUS, *and the
Soothsayer.]*

Caesar
　The ides of March are come.
Soothsayer
　Ay, Caesar, but not gone.
Artemidorus
　Hail, Caesar! Read this schedule.
Decius
　Trebonius doth desire you to o'er-read,
　At your best leisure, this his humble suit.　　　　　　5
Artemidorus
　O Caesar, read mine first; for mine's a suit
　That touches Caesar nearer. Read it, great Caesar.
Caesar
　What touches us ourself shall be last serv'd.
Artemidorus
　Delay not, Caesar; read it instantly.
Caesar
　What, is the fellow mad?
Publius
　　　　　　　　　Sirrah, give place.　　　　　　10
Cassius
　What, urge you your petitions in the street?
　Come to the Capitol.

　　　[CAESAR enters the Capitol, the rest following.]

Popilius
I wish your enterprise to-day may thrive.
Cassius
What enterprise, Popilius?
Popilius

Fare you well.

[Advances to CAESAR.]

Brutus
15 What said Popilius Lena?
Cassius
He wish'd to-day our enterprise might thrive.
I fear our purpose is discovered.
Brutus
Look how he makes to Caesar. Mark him.
Cassius
Casca, be sudden, for we fear prevention.
20 Brutus, what shall be done? If this be known,
Cassius or Caesar never shall turn back,
For I will slay myself.
Brutus

Cassius, be constant.

Popilius Lena speaks not of our purposes;
For look, he smiles, and Caesar doth not change.
Cassius
25 Trebonius knows his time; for look you, Brutus,
He draws Mark Antony out of the way.

[Exeunt ANTONY and TREBONIUS.]

Decius
Where is Metellus Cimber? Let him go
And presently prefer his suit to Caesar.
Brutus
He is address'd; press near and second him.
Cinna
30 Casca, you are the first that rears your hand.

Caesar

    Are we all ready? What is now amiss

    That Caesar and his Senate must redress?

Metellus

    Most high, most mighty, and most puissant Caesar,

    Metellus Cimber throws before thy seat

    An humble heart. *[Kneeling.]*

Caesar

                   I must prevent thee, Cimber.   35

    These couchings and these lowly courtesies

    Might fire the blood of ordinary men,

    And turn pre-ordinance and first decree

    Into the law of children. Be not fond

    To think that Caesar bears such rebel blood   40

    That will be thaw'd from the true quality

    With that which melteth fools – I mean, sweet words,

    Low-crooked curtsies, and base spaniel fawning.

    Thy brother by decree is banished;

    If thou dost bend, and pray, and fawn for him,   45

    I spurn thee like a cur out of my way.

    Know, Caesar doth not wrong; nor without cause

    Will he be satisfied.

Metellus

    Is there no voice more worthy than my own

    To sound more sweetly in great Caesar's ear   50

    For the repealing of my banish'd brother?

Brutus

    I kiss thy hand, but not in flattery, Caesar,

    Desiring thee that Publius Cimber may

    Have an immediate freedom of repeal.

Caesar

    What, Brutus!

Cassius

            Pardon, Caesar! Caesar, pardon!   55

    As low as to thy foot doth Cassius fall,

    To beg enfranchisement for Publius Cimber.

Caesar
> I could be well mov'd, if I were as you;
> If I could pray to move, prayers would move me;
60 But I am constant as the northern star,
> Of whose true-fix'd and resting quality
> There is no fellow in the firmament.
> The skies are painted with unnumb'red sparks,
> They are all fire, and every one doth shine;
65 But there's but one in all doth hold his place.
> So in the world: 'tis furnish'd well with men,
> And men are flesh and blood, and apprehensive;
> Yet in the number I do know but one
> That unassailable holds on his rank,
70 Unshak'd of motion; and that I am he,
> Let me a little show it, even in this –
> That I was constant Cimber should be banish'd,
> And constant do remain to keep him so.

Cinna
> O Caesar!

Caesar
>   Hence! Wilt thou lift up Olympus?

Decius
> Great Caesar!

Caesar
75   Doth not Brutus bootless kneel?

Casca
> Speak, hands, for me!

> *[They stab CAESAR. CASCA strikes the first, BRUTUS the last blow.]*

Caesar
> Et tu, Brute? – Then fall, Caesar!

> *[Dies.]*

Cinna
> Liberty! Freedom! Tyranny is dead!
> Run hence, proclaim, cry it about the streets.

Cassius
    Some to the common pulpits, and cry out   80
    'Liberty, freedom, and enfranchisement!'
Brutus
    People and Senators, be not affrighted.
    Fly not; stand still. Ambition's debt is paid.
Casca
    Go to the pulpit, Brutus.
Decius
    And Cassius too.   85
Brutus
    Where's Publius?
Cinna
    Here, quite confounded with this mutiny.
Metellus
    Stand fast together, lest some friend of Caesar's
    Should chance –
Brutus
    Talk not of standing. Publius, good cheer!   90
    There is no harm intended to your person,
    Nor to no Roman else. So tell them, Publius.
Cassius
    And leave us, Publius, lest that the people,
    Rushing on us, should do your age some mischief.
Brutus
    Do so; and let no man abide this deed   95
    But we the doers.

[Re-enter TREBONIUS.]

Cassius
    Where is Antony?
Trebonius
                Fled to his house amaz'd.
    Men, wives, and children, stare, cry out, and run,
    As it were doomsday.
Brutus
                Fates, we will know your pleasures.

100   That we shall die, we know; 'tis but the time,
       And drawing days out, that men stand upon.

Cassius

       Why, he that cuts off twenty years of life
       Cuts off so many years of fearing death.

Brutus

       Grant that, and then is death a benefit.

105   So are we Caesar's friends, that have abridg'd
       His time of fearing death. Stoop, Romans, stoop,
       And let us bathe our hands in Caesar's blood
       Up to the elbows, and besmear our swords.
       Then walk we forth, even to the marketplace,

110   And waving our red weapons o'er our heads,
       Let's all cry 'Peace, freedom, and liberty!'

Cassius

       Stoop then, and wash. How many ages hence
       Shall this our lofty scene be acted over
       In states unborn and accents yet unknown!

Brutus

115   How many times shall Caesar bleed in sport,
       That now on Pompey's basis lies along
       No worthier than the dust!

Cassius

                      So oft as that shall be,
       So often shall the knot of us be call'd
       The men that gave their country liberty.

Decius

       What, shall we forth?

Cassius

120   Ay, every man away.
       Brutus shall lead, and we will grace his heels
       With the most boldest and best hearts of Rome.

[Enter a Servant.]

Brutus

       Soft, who comes here? A friend of Antony's.

Servant

    Thus, Brutus, did my master bid me kneel;
    Thus did Mark Antony bid me fall down;   125
    And, being prostrate, thus he bade me say:
    Brutus is noble, wise, valiant, and honest;
    Caesar was mighty, bold, royal, and loving.
    Say I love Brutus, and I honour him;
    Say I fear'd Caesar, honour'd him, and lov'd him.   130
    If Brutus will vouchsafe that Antony
    May safely come to him, and be resolv'd
    How Caesar hath deserv'd to lie in death,
    Mark Antony shall not love Caesar dead
    So well as Brutus living; but will follow   135
    The fortunes and affairs of noble Brutus
    Thorough the hazards of this untrod state
    With all true faith. So says my master Antony.

Brutus

    Thy master is a wise and valiant Roman;
    I never thought him worse.   140
    Tell him, so please him come unto this place,
    He shall be satisfied and, by my honour,
    Depart untouch'd.

Servant

               I'll fetch him presently.

[Exit.]

Brutus

    I know that we shall have him well to friend.

Cassius

    I wish we may. But yet have I a mind   145
    That fears him much; and my misgiving still
    Falls shrewdly to the purpose.

[Re-enter ANTONY.]

Brutus

    But here comes Antony. Welcome, Mark Antony.

57

Antony
> O mighty Caesar! dost thou lie so low?
150 Are all thy conquests, glories, triumphs, spoils,
> Shrunk to this little measure? Fare thee well.
> I know not, gentlemen, what you intend,
> Who else must be let blood, who else is rank.
> If I myself, there is no hour so fit
135 As Caesar's death's hour; nor no instrument
> Of half that worth as those your swords, made rich
> With the most noble blood of all this world.
> I do beseech ye, if you bear me hard,
> Now, whilst your purpled hands do reek and smoke,
160 Fulfil your pleasure. Live a thousand years,
> I shall not find myself so apt to die.
> No place will please me so, no mean of death,
> As here by Caesar, and by you cut off,
> The choice and master spirits of this age.

Brutus
165 O Antony! beg not your death of us.
> Though now we must appear bloody and cruel,
> As by our hands and this our present act
> You see we do; yet see you but our hands,
> And this the bleeding business they have done.
170 Our hearts you see not; they are pitiful;
> And pity to the general wrong of Rome,
> As fire drives out fire, so pity pity,
> Hath done this deed on Caesar. For your part,
> To you our swords have leaden points, Mark Antony;
175 Our arms in strength of malice, and our hearts
> Of brothers' temper, do receive you in
> With all kind love, good thoughts, and reverence.

Cassius
> Your voice shall be as strong as any man's
> In the disposing of new dignities.

Brutus
180 Only be patient till we have appeas'd
> The multitude, beside themselves with fear,
> And then we will deliver you the cause

Why I, that did love Caesar when I struck him,
Have thus proceeded.
Antony
       I doubt not of your wisdom.
Let each man render me his bloody hand.   185
First, Marcus Brutus, will I shake with you;
Next, Caius Cassius, do I take your hand;
Now, Decius Brutus, yours; now yours, Metellus;
Yours, Cinna; and, my valiant Casca, yours.
Though last, not least in love, yours, good Trebonius.   190
Gentlemen all – alas, what shall I say?
My credit now stands on such slippery ground
That one of two bad ways you must conceit me,
Either a coward or a flatterer.
That I did love thee, Caesar, O, 'tis true!   195
If then thy spirit look upon us now,
Shall it not grieve thee dearer than thy death
To see thy Antony making his peace,
Shaking the bloody fingers of thy foes,
Most noble! in the presence of thy corse?   200
Had I as many eyes as thou hast wounds,
Weeping as fast as they stream forth thy blood,
It would become me better than to close
In terms of friendship with thine enemies.
Pardon me, Julius! Here wast thou bay'd, brave hart;   205
Here didst thou fall; and here thy hunters stand,
Sign'd in thy spoil, and crimson'd in thy lethe.
O world, thou wast the forest to this hart;
And this indeed, O world, the heart of thee!
How like a deer strucken by many princes   210
Dost thou here lie!
Cassius
Mark Antony –
Antony
      Pardon me, Caius Cassius.
The enemies of Caesar shall say this;
Then, in a friend, it is cold modesty.

Cassius

215   I blame you not for praising Caesar so;
       But what compact mean you to have with us?
       Will you be prick'd in number of our friends,
       Or shall we on, and not depend on you?

Antony

       Therefore I took your hands; but was indeed
220   Sway'd from the point by looking down on Caesar.
       Friends am I with you all, and love you all,
       Upon this hope, that you shall give me reasons
       Why and wherein Caesar was dangerous.

Brutus

       Or else were this a savage spectacle.
225   Our reasons are so full of good regard
       That were you, Antony, the son of Caesar,
       You should be satisfied.

Antony

                  That's all I seek;
       And am moreover suitor that I may
       Produce his body to the market-place
230   And, in the pulpit, as becomes a friend,
       Speak in the order of his funeral.

Brutus

       You shall, Mark Antony.

Cassius

                Brutus, a word with you.

[Aside to BRUTUS*]*

       You know not what you do. Do not consent
       That Antony speak in his funeral.
235   Know you how much the people may be mov'd
       By that which he will utter?

Brutus

       [Aside to CASSIUS*]* By your pardon –
       I will myself into the pulpit first,
       And show the reason of our Caesar's death.
       What Antony shall speak, I will protest
240   He speaks by leave and by permission;

And that we are contented Caesar shall
Have all true rites and lawful ceremonies.
It shall advantage more than do us wrong.

Cassius

I know not what may fall. I like it not.

Brutus

Mark Antony, here, take you Caesar's body.   245
You shall not in your funeral speech blame us,
But speak all good you can devise of Caesar;
And say you do't by our permission;
Else shall you not have any hand at all
About his funeral. And you shall speak   250
In the same pulpit whereto I am going,
After my speech is ended.

Antony

                    Be it so;
I do desire no more.

Brutus

Prepare the body then, and follow us.

[Exeunt all but ANTONY.]

Antony

O, pardon me, thou bleeding piece of earth,   255
That I am meek and gentle with these butchers!
Thou art the ruins of the noblest man
That ever lived in the tide of times.
Woe to the hand that shed this costly blood!
Over thy wounds now do I prophesy –   260
Which like dumb mouths do ope their ruby lips
To beg the voice and utterance of my tongue –
A curse shall light upon the limbs of men;
Domestic fury and fierce civil strife
Shall cumber all the parts of Italy;   265
Blood and destruction shall be so in use,
And dreadful objects so familiar,
That mothers shall but smile when they behold
Their infants quartered with the hands of war,

270   All pity chok'd with custom of fell deeds;
And Caesar's spirit, ranging for revenge,
With Até by his side come hot from hell,
Shall in these confines with a monarch's voice
Cry 'Havoc!' and let slip the dogs of war,
That this foul deed shall smell above the earth
With carrion men, groaning for burial.

[Enter Octavius' Servant.]

You serve Octavius Caesar, do you not?
Servant
I do, Mark Antony.
Antony
Caesar did write for him to come to Rome.
Servant
280   He did receive his letters, and is coming,
And bid me say to you by word of mouth –
O Caesar! *[Seeing the body.]*
Antony
Thy heart is big, get thee apart and weep.
Passion, I see, is catching; for mine eyes,
285   Seeing those beads of sorrow stand in thine,
Began to water. Is thy master coming?
Servant
He lies to-night within seven leagues of Rome.
Antony
Post back with speed, and tell him what hath chanc'd.
Here is a mourning Rome, a dangerous Rome,
290   No Rome of safety for Octavius yet;
Hie hence and tell him so. Yet stay awhile;
Thou shalt not back till I have borne this corse
to the market-place. There shall I try,
In my oration, how the people take
295   The cruel issue of these bloody men;
According to the which thou shalt discourse
To young Octavius of the state of things.
Lend me your hand.

[Exeunt with Caesar's body.]

Scene II

Rome. The Forum.

[Enter BRUTUS and CASSIUS, with the Plebeians.]

Citizens
We will be satisfied! Let us be satisfied!
Brutus
Then follow me, and give me audience, friends.
Cassius, go you into the other street,
And part the numbers.
Those that will hear me speak, let 'em stay here;   5
Those that will follow Cassius, go with him;
And public reasons shall be rendered
Of Caesar's death.
1 Plebeian
             I will hear Brutus speak.
2 Plebeian
I will hear Cassius, and compare their reasons,
When severally we hear them rendered.   10

*[Exit CASSIUS, with some of the Plebeians. BRUTUS goes
into the pulpit.]*

3 Plebeian
The noble Brutus is ascended. Silence!
Brutus
Be patient till the last.
Romans, countrymen, and lovers! hear me for my
cause, and be silent, that you may hear. Believe me
for mine honour, and have respect to mine honour,   15
that you may believe. Censure me in your wisdom,
and awake your senses, that you may the better judge.
If there be any in this assembly, any dear friend of
Caesar's, to him I say that Brutus' love to Caesar was no
less than his. If then that friend demand why Brutus   20
rose against Caesar, this is my answer: Not that I lov'd
Caesar less, but that I lov'd Rome more. Had you rather

Caesar were living, and die all slaves, than that Caesar
were dead, to live all free men? As Caesar lov'd me, I
25   weep for him; as he was fortunate, I rejoice at it; as he
was valiant, I honour him; but – as he was ambitious, I
slew him. There is tears for his love; joy for his fortune;
honour for his valour; and death for his ambition.
Who is here so base that would be a bondman? If any,
30   speak; for him have I offended. Who is here so rude
that would not be a Roman? If any, speak; for him have
I offended. Who is here so vile that will not love his
country? If any, speak; for him have I offended. I pause
for a reply.

All

35   None, Brutus, none.

Brutus

Then none have I offended. I have done no more
to Caesar than you shall do to Brutus. The question
of his death is enroll'd in the Capitol; his glory not
extenuated, wherein he was worthy; nor his offences
40   enforc'd, for which he suffered death.

[Enter ANTONY and Others with Caesar's body.]

Here comes his body, mourn'd by Mark Antony, who,
though he had no hand in his death, shall receive the
benefit of his dying, a place in the commonwealth,
as which of you shall not? With this I depart, that,
45   as I slew my best lover for the good of Rome, I have
the same dagger for myself, when it shall please my
country to need my death.

All

Live, Brutus! live, live!

1 Plebeian

Bring him with triumph home unto his house.

2 Plebeian

50   Give him a statue with his ancestors.

3 Plebeian

Let him be Caesar.

4 Plebeian

                       Caesar's better parts
   Shall be crown'd in Brutus.

1 Plebeian

   We'll bring him to his house with shouts and
      clamours.

Brutus

   My countrymen –

2 Plebeian

                   Peace, silence! Brutus speaks.

1 Plebeian

   Peace, ho!   55

Brutus

   Good countrymen, let me depart alone,
   And for my sake stay here with Antony.
   Do grace to Caesar's corpse, and grace his speech
   Tending to Caesar's glories, which Mark Antony,
   By our permission, is allow'd to make.   60
   I do entreat you, not a man depart
   Save I alone, till Antony have spoke. *[Exit.]*

1 Plebeian

   Stay, ho! and let us hear Mark Antony.

3 Plebeian

   Let him go up into the public chair.
   We'll hear him. Noble Antony, go up.   65

Antony

   For Brutus' sake I am beholding to you.

                  [Goes up.]

4 Plebeian

   What does he say of Brutus?

3 Plebeian

                       He says, for Brutus' sake
   He finds himself beholding to us all.

4 Plebeian

   'Twere best he speak no harm of Brutus here.

1 Plebeian
This Caesar was a tyrant.
3 Plebeian
70   Nay, that's certain.
We are blest that Rome is rid of him.
2 Plebeian
Peace! let us hear what Antony can say.
Antony
You gentle Romans –
All
                                 Peace, ho! let us hear him.
Antony
Friends, Romans, countrymen, lend me your ears;
75   I come to bury Caesar, not to praise him.
The evil that men do lives after them;
The good is oft interred with their bones;
So let it be with Caesar. The noble Brutus
Hath told you Caesar was ambitious.
80   If it were so, it was a grievous fault;
And grievously hath Caesar answer'd it.
Here, under leave of Brutus and the rest –
For Brutus is an honourable man;
So are they all, all honourable men –
85   Come I to speak in Caesar's funeral.
He was my friend, faithful and just to me;
But Brutus says he was ambitious,
And Brutus is an honourable man.
He hath brought many captives home to Rome,
90   Whose ransoms did the general coffers fill;
Did this in Caesar seem ambitious?
When that the poor have cried, Caesar hath wept;
Ambition should be made of sterner stuff.
Yet Brutus says he was ambitious;
95   And Brutus is an honourable man.
You all did see that on the Lupercal
I thrice presented him a kingly crown,
Which he did thrice refuse. Was this ambition?

Yet Brutus says he was ambitious;
And sure he is an honourable man.   100
I speak not to disprove what Brutus spoke,
But here I am to speak what I do know.
You all did love him once, not without cause;
What cause withholds you, then, to mourn for him?
O judgment, thou art fled to brutish beasts,   105
And men have lost their reason! Bear with me;
My heart is in the coffin there with Caesar,
And I must pause till it come back to me.

1 Plebeian

Methinks there is much reason in his sayings.

2 Plebeian

If thou consider rightly of the matter,   110
Caesar has had great wrong.

3 Plebeian

                        Has he, masters!
I fear there will a worse come in his place.

4 Plebeian

Mark'd ye his words? He would not take the crown;
Therefore 'tis certain he was not ambitious.

1 Plebeian

If it be found so, some will dear abide it.   115

2 Plebeian

Poor soul! his eyes are red as fire with weeping.

3 Plebeian

There's not a nobler man in Rome than Antony.

4 Plebeian

Now mark him, he begins again to speak.

Antony

But yesterday the word of Caesar might
Have stood against the world: now lies he there,   120
And none so poor to do him reverence.
O masters, if I were dispos'd to stir
Your hearts and minds to mutiny and rage,
I should do Brutus wrong, and Cassius wrong,
Who, you all know, are honourable men.   125

I will not do them wrong; I rather choose
To wrong the dead, to wrong myself and you,
Than I will wrong such honourable men.
But here's a parchment with the seal of Caesar;
130   I found it in his closet –'tis his will.
Let but the commons hear this testament,
Which, pardon me, I do not mean to read,
And they would go and kiss dead Caesar's wounds
And dip their napkins in his sacred blood;
135   Yea, beg a hair of him for memory
And, dying, mention it within their wills,
Bequeathing it as a rich legacy
Unto their issue.

4 Plebeian

We'll hear the will. Read it, Mark Antony.

All

140   The will, the will! We will hear Caesar's will.

Antony

Have patience, gentle friends, I must not read it;
It is not meet you know how Caesar lov'd you.
You are not wood, you are not stones, but men;
And being men, hearing the will of Caesar,
145   It will inflame you, it will make you mad.
'Tis good you know not that you are his heirs;
For if you should, O, what would come of it?

4 Plebeian

Read the will; we'll hear it, Antony!
You shall read us the will – Caesar's will.

Antony

150   Will you be patient? Will you stay awhile?
I have o'ershot myself to tell you of it.
I fear I wrong the honourable men
Whose daggers have stabb'd Caesar; I do fear it.

4 Plebeian

They were traitors. Honourable men!

All

155   The will! the testament!

2 Plebeian

 They were villains, murderers.

 The will! Read the will.

Antony

 You will compel me, then, to read the will?

 Then make a ring about the corpse of Caesar,

 And let me show you him that made the will. 160

 Shall I descend? and will you give me leave?

All

 Come down.

2 Plebeian

     Descend. *[ANTONY comes down.]*

3 Plebeian

 You shall have leave.

4 Plebeian

 A ring! Stand round.

1 Plebeian

 Stand from the hearse, stand from the body. 165

2 Plebeian

 Room for Antony, most noble Antony!

Antony

 Nay, press not so upon me; stand far off.

All

 Stand back. Room! Bear back.

Antony

 If you have tears, prepare to shed them now.

 You all do know this mantle. I remember 170

 The first time ever Caesar put it on;

 'Twas on a summer's evening, in his tent,

 That day he overcame the Nervii.

 Look! in this place ran Cassius' dagger through;

 See what a rent the envious Casca made; 175

 Through this the well-beloved Brutus stabb'd,

 And as he pluck'd his cursed steel away,

 Mark how the blood of Caesar follow'd it,

 As rushing out of doors, to be resolv'd

 If Brutus so unkindly knock'd or no; 180

For Brutus, as you know, was Caesar's angel.
Judge, O you gods, how dearly Caesar lov'd him!
This was the most unkindest cut of all;
For when the noble Caesar saw him stab,
185 Ingratitude, more strong than traitors' arms,
Quite vanquish'd him. Then burst his mighty heart;
And in his mantle muffling up his face,
Even at the base of Pompey's statua,
Which all the while ran blood, great Caesar fell.
190 O, what a fall was there, my countrymen!
Then I, and you, and all of us fell down,
Whilst bloody treason flourish'd over us.
O, now you weep, and I perceive you fell
The din't of pity. These are gracious drops.
195 Kind souls, what weep you when you but behold
Our Caesar's vesture wounded? Look you here,
Here is himself, marr'd as you see with traitors.

1 Plebeian

O piteous spectacle!

2 Plebeian

O noble Caesar!

3 Plebeian

200 O woeful day!

4 Plebeian

O traitors, villains!

1 Plebeian

O most bloody sight!

2 Plebeian

We will be reveng'd.

All

Revenge! About! Seek! Burn! Fire! Kill! Slay!
205 Let not a traitor live!

Antony

Stay, countrymen.

1 Plebeian

Peace there! Hear the noble Antony.

Plebeian
> We'll hear him, we'll follow him, we'll die with him.

Antony
> Good friends, sweet friends, let me not stir you up
> To such a sudden flood of mutiny.   210
> They that have done this deed are honourable.
> What private griefs they have, alas, I know not,
> That made them do it; they are wise and honourable,
> And will, no doubt, with reasons answer you.
> I come not, friends, to steal away your hearts;   215
> I am no orator, as Brutus is,
> But, as you know me all, a plain blunt man,
> That love my friend; and that they know full well
> That gave me public leave to speak of him.
> For I have neither wit, nor words, nor worth,   220
> Action, nor utterance, nor the power of speech,
> To stir men's blood; I only speak right on.
> I tell you that which you yourselves do know;
> Show you sweet Caesar's wounds, poor poor dumb
>   mouths,
> And bid them speak for me. But were I Brutus,   225
> And Brutus Antony, there were an Antony
> Would ruffle up your spirits, and put a tongue
> In every wound of Caesar, that should move
> The stones of Rome to rise and mutiny.

All
> We'll mutiny.   230

1 Plebeian
> We'll burn the house of Brutus.

3 Plebeian
> Away, then! Come seek the conspirators.

Antony
> Yet hear me, countrymen; yet hear me speak.

All
> Peace, ho! Hear Antony, most noble Antony.

Antony
> Why, friends, you go to do you know not what.   235

Wherein hath Caesar thus deserv'd your loves?
Alas, you know not! I must tell you, then:
You have forgot the will I told you of.

All

Most true. The will! Let's stay and hear the will.

Antony

240   Here is the will, and under Caesar's seal:
To every Roman citizen he gives,
To every several man, seventy-five drachmas.

2 Plebeian

Most noble Caesar! We'll revenge his death.

Plebeian

O royal Caesar!

Antony

245   Hear me with patience.

All

Peace, ho!

Antony

Moreover, he hath left you all his walks,
His private arbours, and new-planted orchards,
On this side Tiber; he hath left them you,

250   And to your heirs for ever – common pleasures,
To walk abroad and recreate yourselves.
Here was a Caesar! When comes such another?

1 Plebeian

Never, never! Come away, away!
We'll burn his body in the holy place,

255   And with the brands fire the traitors' houses.
Take up the body.

2 Plebeian

Go, fetch fire.

3 Plebeian

Pluck down benches.

4 Plebeian

Pluck down forms, windows, any thing. *[Exeunt
Plebeians with the body.]*

Antony

    Now let it work. Mischief, thou art afoot,   260
    Take thou what course thou wilt.

[Enter a Servant.]

                         How now, fellow!

Servant

    Sir, Octavius is already come to Rome.

Antony

    Where is he?

Servant

    He and Lepidus are at Caesar's house.

Antony

    And thither will I straight to visit him.   265
    He comes upon a wish. Fortune is merry,
    And in this mood will give us any thing.

Servant

    I heard him say Brutus and Cassius
    Are rid like madmen through the gates of Rome.

Antony

    Belike they had some notice of the people,   270
    How I had mov'd them. Bring me to Octavius.

[Exeunt.]

Scene III

Rome. A street.

[Enter CINNA *the Poet, and after him the Plebeians.]*

Cinna
I dreamt to-night that I did feast with Caesar,
And things unluckily charge my fantasy.
I have no will to wander forth of doors,
Yet something leads me forth.

1 Plebeian
5 What is your name?

2 Plebeian
Whither are you going?

3 Plebeian
Where do you dwell?

4 Plebeian
Are you a married man or a bachelor?

2 Plebeian
Answer every man directly.

1 Plebeian
10 Ay, and briefly.

4 Plebeian
Ay, and wisely.

3 Plebeian
Ay, and truly, you were best.

Cinna
What is my name? Whither am I going? Where do
I dwell? Am I a married man or a bachelor? Then to
15 answer every man directly and briefly, wisely and truly:
wisely, I say I am a bachelor.

2 Plebeian
That's as much as to say they are fools that marry.
You'll bear me a bang for that, I fear. Proceed directly.

Cinna
Directly, I am going to Caesar's funeral.

1 Plebeian

As a friend or an enemy? 20

Cinna

As a friend.

2 Plebeian

That matter is answered directly.

4 Plebeian

For your dwelling – briefly.

Cinna

Briefly, I dwell by the Capitol.

3 Plebeian

Your name, sir, truly. 25

Cinna

Truly, my name is Cinna.

1 Plebeian

Tear him to pieces; he's a conspirator!

Cinna

I am Cinna the poet, I am Cinna the poet.

4 Plebeian

Tear him for his bad verses, tear him for his bad verses!

Cinna

I am not Cinna the conspirator. 30

4 Plebeian

It is no matter, his name's Cinna; pluck but his name out of his heart, and turn him going.

3 Plebeian

Tear him, tear him! Come, brands, ho! fire-brands! To Brutus', to Cassius'! Burn all! Some to Decius' house, and some to Casca's; some to Ligarius'. Away, go! 35

[Exeunt all the Plebeians with CINNA.*]*

ACT FOUR

Scene I

Rome. Antony's house.

[Enter ANTONY, OCTAVIUS, and LEPIDUS.]

Antony
These many, then, shall die; their names are prick'd.
Octavius
Your brother too must die. Consent you, Lepidus?
Lepidus
I do consent.
Octavius
           Prick him down, Antony.
Lepidus
Upon condition Publius shall not live,
5 Who is your sister's son, Mark Antony.
Antony
He shall not live; look, with a spot I damn him.
But, Lepidus, go you to Caesar's house;
Fetch the will hither, and we shall determine
How to cut off some charge in legacies.
Lepidus
10 What, shall I find you here?
Octavius
Or here or at the Capitol.

[Exit LEPIDUS.]

Antony
This is a slight unmeritable man,
Meet to be sent on errands. Is it fit,
The threefold world divided, he should stand
One of the three to share it?
Octavius
15   So you thought him,

And took his voice who should be prick'd to die
In our black sentence and proscription.

Antony

Octavius, I have seen more days than you;
And though we lay these honours on this man,
To ease ourselves of divers sland'rous loads,   20
He shall but bear them as the ass bears gold,
The groan and sweat under the business,
Either led or driven as we point the way;
And having brought our treasure where we will,
Then take we down his load, and turn him off,   25
Like to the empty ass, to shake his ears
And graze in commons.

Octavius

                     You may do your will;
But he's a tried and valiant soldier.

Antony

So is my horse, Octavius, and for that
I do appoint him store of provender.   30
It is a creature that I teach to fight,
To wind, to stop, to run directly on,
His corporal motion govern'd by my spirit.
And, in some taste, is Lepidus but so:
He must be taught, and train'd, and bid go forth;   35
A barren-spirited fellow; one that feeds
On abjects, orts, and imitations,
Which, out of use and stal'd by other men,
Begin his fashion. Do not talk of him
But as a property. And now, Octavius,   40
Listen great things: Brutus and Cassius
Are levying powers; we must straight make head;
Therefore let our alliance be combin'd,
Our best friends made, our means stretch'd;
And let us presently go sit in council   45
How covert matters may be best disclos'd,
And open perils surest answered.

Octavius
Let us do so; for we are at the stake,
And bay'd about with many enemies;
50   And some that smile have in their hearts, I fear,
Millions of mischiefs.

[Exeunt.]

Scene II

The Camp near Sardis. Before the tent of Brutus.

[Drum. Enter BRUTUS, LUCILIUS, LUCIUS, *and the Army.*
TITINIUS *and* PINDARUS *meet them.]*

Brutus
    Stand, ho!
Lucilius
    Give the word, ho! and stand.
Brutus
    What now, Lucilius? Is Cassius near?
Lucilius
    He is at hand, and Pindarus is come
    To do you salutation from his master. 5
Brutus
    He greets me well. Your master, Pindarus,
    In his own change, or by ill officers,
    Hath given me some worthy cause to wish
    Things done undone; but if he be at hand
    I shall be satisfied.
Pindarus
                I do not doubt 10
    But that my noble master will appear
    Such as he is, full of regard and honour.
Brutus
    He is not doubted. A word, Lucilius,
    How he receiv'd you; let me be resolv'd.
Lucilius
    With courtesy and with respect enough, 15
    But not with such familiar instances
    Nor with such free and friendly conference
    As he hath us'd of old.
Brutus
              Thou hast describ'd
    A hot friend cooling. Ever note, Lucillius,
    When love begins to sicken and decay, 20

It useth an enforced ceremony.
There are no tricks in plain and simple faith;
But hollow men, like horses hot at hand,
Make gallant show and promise of their mettle;
25   But when they should endure the bloody spur,
They fall their crests, and like deceitful jades
Sink in the trial. Comes his army on?

Lucilius

They mean this night in Sardis to be quarter'd.
The greater part, the horse in general,
Are come with Cassius. *[Low march within.]*

Brutus

30   Hark! he is arriv'd:
March gently on to meet him.

[Enter CASSIUS *and his Powers.]*

Cassius

Stand, ho!

Brutus

Stand, ho! Speak the word along.

1 Soldier

Stand!

2 Soldier

35   Stand!

3 Soldier

Stand!

Cassius

Most noble brother, you have done me wrong.

Brutus

Judge me, you gods! wrong I mine enemies?
And, if not so, how should I wrong a brother?

Cassius

40   Brutus, this sober form of yours hides wrongs;
And when you do them –

Brutus

                    Cassius, be content;
Speak your griefs softly; I do know you well.

Before the eyes of both our armies here,
Which should perceive nothing but love from us,
Let us not wrangle. Bid them move away;   45
Then in my tent, Cassius, enlarge your griefs,
And I will give you audience.

Cassius

                    Pindarus,
Bid our commanders lead their charges off
A little from this ground.

Brutus

Lucilius, do you the like; and let no man   50
Come to our tent till we have done our conference.
Let Lucius and Titinius guard our door.

[Exeunt.]

Scene III

The Camp near Sardis. Within the tent of Brutus.

[Enter BRUTUS *and* CASSIUS.*]*

Cassius
> That you have wrong'd me doth appear in this:
> You have condemn'd and noted Lucius Pella
> For taking bribes here of the Sardians;
> Wherein my letters, praying on his side,
> 5 Because I knew the man, were slighted off.

Brutus
> You wrong'd yourself to write in such a case.

Cassius
> In such a time as this it is not meet
> That every nice offence should bear his comment.

Brutus
> Let me tell you, Cassius, you yourself
> 10 Are much condemn'd to have an itching palm,
> To sell and mart your offices for gold
> To undeservers.

Cassius
> I an itching palm!
> You know that you are Brutus that speaks this,
> Or, by the gods, this speech were else your last.

Brutus
> 15 The name of Cassius honours this corruption,
> And chastisement doth therefore hide his head.

Cassius
> Chastisement!

Brutus
> Remember March, the ides of March remember:
> Did not great Julius bleed for justice sake?
> 20 What villian touch'd his body, that did stab,
> And not for justice? What, shall one of us,
> That struck the foremost man of all this world
> But for supporting robbers, shall we now

Contaminate our fingers with base bribes,
And sell the mighty space of our large honours   25
For so much trash as may be grasped thus?
I had rather be a dog and bay the moon
Than such a Roman.

Cassius

        Brutus, bait not me!
I'll not endure it. You forget yourself,
To hedge me in. I am a soldier, I,   30
Older in practice, abler than yourself
To make conditions.

Brutus

        Go to; you are not, Cassius.

Cassius

I am.

Brutus

I say you are not.

Cassius

Urge me no more, I shall forget myself;   35
Have mind upon your health, tempt me no farther.

Brutus

Away, slight man!

Cassius

Is't possible?

Brutus

        Hear me, for I will speak.
Must I give way and room to your rash choler?
Shall I be frighted when a madman stares?   40

Cassius

O ye gods, ye gods! must I endure all this?

Brutus

All this? Ay, more! Fret till your proud heart break.
Go show your slaves how choleric you are,
And make your bondmen tremble. Must I budge?
Must I observe you? Must I stand and crouch   45
Under your testy humour? By the gods,
You shall digest the venom of your spleen

Though it do split you; for from this day forth
I'll use you for my mirth, yea, for my laughter,
When you are waspish.

Cassius

50   Is it come to this?

Brutus

You say you are a better soldier.
Let it appear so; make your vaunting true,
And it shall please me well. For mine own part,
I shall be glad to learn of noble men.

Cassius

55   You wrong me every way; you wrong me, Brutus;
I said an elder soldier, not a better.
Did I say 'better'?

Brutus

                            If you did, I care not.

Cassius

When Caesar liv'd, he durst not thus have mov'd me.

Brutus

Peace, peace! You durst not so have tempted him.

Cassius

60   I durst not?

Brutus

No.

Cassius

What, durst not tempt him?

Brutus

                                        For your life you durst not.

Cassius

Do not presume too much upon my love;
I may do that I shall be sorry for.

Brutus

65   You have done that you should be sorry for.
There is no terror, Cassius, in your threats;
For I am arm'd so strong in honesty
That they pass by me as the idle wind,
Which I respect not. I did send to you

For certain sums of gold, which you denied me;   70
For I can raise no money by vile means.
By heaven, I had rather coin my heart,
And drop my blood for drachmas, than to wring
From the hard hands of peasants their vile trash
By any indirection. I did send   75
To you for gold to pay my legions,
Which you denied me; was that done like Cassius?
Should I have answer'd Caius Cassius so?
When Marcus Brutus grows so covetous,
To lock such rascal counters from his friends,   80
Be ready, gods, with all your thunderbolts,
Dash him to pieces!

Cassius

             I denied you not.

Brutus

  You did.

Cassius

         I did not. He was but a fool
That brought my answer back.
Brutus hath riv'd my heart.   85
A friend should bear his friend's infirmities,
But Brutus makes mine greater than they are.

Brutus

  I do not, till you practise them on me.

Cassius

  You love me not.

Brutus

         I do not like your faults.

Cassius

  A friendly eye could never see such faults.   90

Brutus

  A flatterer's would not, though they do appear
As huge as high Olympus.

Cassius

  Come, Antony, and young Octavius, come,
Revenge yourselves alone on Cassius,

95   For Cassius is aweary of the world:
Hated by one he loves; brav'd by his brother;
Check'd like a bondman; all his faults observ'd,
Set in a notebook, learn'd, and conn'd by rote,
To cast into my teeth. O, I could weep
100   My spirit from mine eyes! There is my dagger,
And here my naked breast; within, a heart
Dearer than Plutus' mine, richer than gold;
If that thou be'st a Roman, take it forth.
I, that denied thee gold, will give my heart.
105   Strike as thou didst at Caesar; for I know,
When thou didst hate him worst, thou lov'dst him better
Than ever thou lov'dst Cassius.

Brutus

                      Sheathe your dagger.
Be angry when you will, it shall have scope;
Do what you will, dishonour shall be humour.
110   O Cassius, you are yoked with a lamb,
That carries anger as the flint bears fire;
Who, much enforced, shows a hasty spark,
And straight is cold again.

Cassius

                    Hath Cassius liv'd
To be but mirth and laughter to his Brutus,
115   When grief and blood ill-temper'd vexeth him?

Brutus

When I spoke that I was ill-temper'd too.

Cassius

Do you confess so much? Give me your hand.

Brutus

And my heart too.

Cassius

                O Brutus!

Brutus

                What's the matter?

Cassius

    Have not you love enough to bear with me,

    When that rash humour which my mother gave me   120

    Makes me forgetful?

Brutus

    Yes, Cassius; and from henceforth,

    When you are over-earnest with your Brutus,

    He'll think your mother chides, and leave you so.

    [Enter a Poet, followed by LUCILIUS, TITINIUS, *and*
    LUCIUS.]*

Poet

    Let me go in to see the generals.   125

    There is some grudge between 'em; 'tis not meet

    They be alone.

Lucilius

    You shall not come to them.

Poet

    Nothing but death shall stay me.

Cassius

    How now! What's the matter?   130

Poet

    For shame, you generals! What do you mean?

    Love, and be friends, as two such men should be;

    For I have seen more years, I'm sure, than ye.

Cassius

    Ha, ha! How vilely doth this cynic rhyme!

Brutus

    Get you hence, sirrah; saucy fellow, hence!   135

Cassius

    Bear with him, Brutus: 'tis his fashion.

Brutus

    I'll know his humour when he knows his time.

    What should the wars do with these jigging fools?

    Companion, hence!

Cassius

                  Away, away, be gone!

[Exit Poet.]

Brutus

140   Lucilius and Titinius, bid the commanders
      Prepare to lodge their companies to-night.

Cassius

      And come yourselves, and bring Messala with you
      Immediately to us.

[Exeunt LUCILIUS *and* TITINIUS.*]*

Brutus

                Lucius, a bowl of wine!

[Exit LUCIUS.*]*

Cassius

      I did not think you could have been so angry.

Brutus

145   O Cassius, I am sick of many griefs!

Cassius

      Of your philosophy you make no use,
      If you give place to accidental evils.

Brutus

      No man bears sorrow better. Portia is dead.

Cassius

      Ha! Portia?

Brutus

150   She is dead.

Cassius

      How scap'd I killing when I cross'd you so?
      O insupportable and touching loss!
      Upon what sickness?

Brutus

                Impatient of my absence,
      And grief that young Octavius with Mark Antony

155   Have made themselves so strong; for with her death
      That tidings came. With this she fell distract,
      And, her attendants absent, swallow'd fire.

Cassius
    And died so?
Brutus
    Even so?
Cassius
    O ye immortal gods!   160

[Enter LUCIUS *with wine and tapers.]*

Brutus
    Speak no more of her. Give me a bowl of wine.
    In this I bury all unkindness, Cassius. *[Drinks.]*
Cassius
    My heart is thirsty for that noble pledge.
    Fill, Lucius, till the wine o'erswell the cup;
    I cannot drink too much of Brutus' love.   165

[Drinks. Exit LUCIUS.*]*

[Re-enter TITINIUS, *with* MESSALA.*]*

Brutus
    Come in, Titinius! Welcome, good Messala!
    Now sit we close about this taper here,
    And call in question our necessities.
Cassius
    Portia, art thou gone?
Brutus
                 No more, I pray you.
    Messala, I have here received letters,   170
    That young Octavius and Mark Antony
    Come down upon us with a mighty power,
    Bending their expedition toward Philippi.
Messala
    Myself have letters of the self-same tenour.
Brutus
    With what addition?   175
Messala
    That, by proscription and bills of outlawry,

Octavius, Antony, and Lepidus,
Have put to death an hundred senators.
Brutus
Therein our letters do not well agree;
180 Mine speak of seventy senators that died
By their proscriptions, Cicero being one.
Cassius
Cicero one!
Messala
                    Cicero is dead,
And by that order of proscription.
Had you your letters from your wife, my lord?
Brutus
185 No, Messala.
Messala
Nor nothing in your letters writ of her?
Brutus
Nothing, Messala.
Messala
                         That, methinks is strange.
Brutus
Why ask you? Hear you aught of her in yours?
Messala
No, my lord.
Brutus
190 Now, as you are a Roman, tell me true.
Messala
Then like a Roman bear the truth I tell:
For certain she is dead, and by strange manner.
Brutus
Why, farewell, Portia. We must die, Messala.
With meditating that she must die once,
195 I have the patience to endure it now.
Messala
Even so great men great losses should endure.
Cassius
I have as much of this in art as you,
But yet my nature could not bear it so.

Brutus

    Well, to our work alive. What do you think

    Of marching to Philippi presently?   200

Cassius

    I do not think it good.

Brutus

                    Your reason?

Cassius

                        This it is:

    'Tis better that the enemy seek us;

    So shall he waste his means, weary his soldiers,

    Doing himself offence, whilst we, lying still,

    Are full of rest, defence, and nimbleness.   205

Brutus

    Good reasons must, of force, give place to better.

    The people 'twixt Philippi and this ground

    Do stand but in a forc'd affection;

    For they have grudg'd us contribution.

    The enemy, marching along by them,   210

    By them shall make a fuller number up,

    Come on refresh'd, new-added, and encourag'd;

    From which advantage shall we cut him off,

    If at Philippi we do face him there,

    These people at our back.

Cassius

                Hear me, good brother.   215

Brutus

    Under your pardon. You must note beside

    That we have tried the utmost of our friends,

    Our legions are brim full, our cause is ripe.

    The enemy increaseth every day:

    We, at the height, are ready to decline.   220

    There is a tide in the affairs of men

    Which, taken at the flood, leads on to fortune;

    Omitted, all the voyage of their life

    Is bound in shallows and in miseries.

    On such a full sea are we now afloat,   225

And we must take the current when it serves,
Or lose our ventures.

Cassius

              Then, with your will, go on;
We'll along ourselves and meet them at Philippi.

Brutus

The deep of night is crept upon our talk,
230   And nature must obey necessity,
Which we will niggard with a little rest.
There is no more to say?

Cassius

              No more. Good night:
Early to-morrow will we rise, and hence.

Brutus

Lucius! *[Enter* LUCIUS*]* My gown.

[Exit LUCIUS*]*

              Farewell, good Messala.
235   Good night, Titinius. Noble, noble Cassius,
Good night, and good repose!

Cassius

              O my dear brother,
This was an ill beginning of the night!
Never come such division 'tween our souls!
Let it not, Brutus.

Brutus

           Everything is well.

Cassius

Good night, my lord.

Brutus

240   Good night, good brother.

Titinius and Messala

Good night, Lord Brutus.

Brutus

           Farewell, every one.

[Exeunt CASSIUS, TITINIUS, *and* MESSALA.*]*

[Re-enter LUCIUS with the gown.]

Give me the gown. Where is thy instrument?
Lucius
    Here in the tent.
Brutus
                What, thou speak'st drowsily?
    Poor knave, I blame thee not; thou art o'erwatch'd.
    Call Claudius and some other of my men;   245
    I'll have them sleep on cushions in my tent.
Lucius
    Varro and Claudius!

[Enter VARRO and CLAUDIUS.]

Varro
    Calls my lord?
Brutus
    I pray you, sirs, lie in my tent and sleep;
    It may be I shall raise you by and by   250
    On business to my brother Cassius.
Varro
    So please you we will stand and watch your pleasure.
Brutus
    I will not have it so. Lie down, good sirs;
    It may be I shall otherwise bethink me.
    Look, Lucius, here's the book I sought for so;   255
    I put it in the pocket of my gown.

[VARRO and CLAUDIUS lie down.]

Lucius
    I was sure your lordship did not give it me.
Brutus
    Bear with me, good boy, I am much forgetful.
    Canst thou hold up thy heavy eyes awhile,
    And touch thy instrument a strain or two?   260
Lucius
    Ay, my lord, an't please you.

Brutus
　　It does, my boy.
　　I trouble thee too much, but thou art willing.
Lucius
　　It is my duty, sir.
Brutus
265　　I should not urge thy duty past thy might;
　　I know young bloods look for a time of rest.
Lucius
　　I have slept, my lord, already.
Brutus
　　It was well done; and thou shalt sleep again;
　　I will not hold thee long. If I do live,
270　　I will be good to thee.

　　　　[Music and a song. LUCIUS falls asleep.]

　　This is a sleepy tune. O murd'rous slumber!
　　Layest thou thy leaden mace upon my boy,
　　That plays thee music? Gentle knave, good night.
　　I will not do thee so much wrong to wake thee.
275　　If thou dost nod, thou break'st thy instrument;
　　I'll take it from thee; and, good boy, good night.
　　Let me see, let me see; is not the leaf turn'd down
　　Where I left reading? Here it is, I think. *[Sits down.]*

　　　　[Enter the Ghost of CAESAR.]

　　How ill this taper burns! Ha! who comes here?
280　　I think it is the weakness of mine eyes
　　That shapes this monstrous apparition.
　　It comes upon me. Art thou any thing?
　　Art thou some god, some angel, or some devil,
　　That mak'st my blood cold and my hair to stare?
285　　Speak to me what thou art.
Ghost
　　Thy evil spirit, Brutus.
Brutus
　　　　　　　　Why com'st thou?

Ghost

  To tell thee thou shalt see me at Philippi.

Brutus

  Well; then I shall see thee again?

Ghost

  Ay, at Philippi.

Brutus

  Why, I will see thee at Philippi, then. *[Exit Ghost.]*   290
  Now I have taken heart thou vanishest.
  Ill spirit, I would hold more talk with thee.
  Boy! Lucius! Varro! Claudius! Sirs, awake! Claudius!

Lucius

  The strings, my lord, are false.

Brutus

  He thinks he still is at his instrument.   295
  Lucius, awake!

Lucius

  My lord!

Brutus

  Didst thou dream, Lucius, that thou so criedst out?

Lucius

  My lord, I do not know that I did cry.

Brutus

  Yes, that thou didst. Didst thou see any thing?   300

Lucius

  Nothing, my lord.

Brutus

  Sleep again, Lucius. Sirrah Claudius! *[To* VARRO*]* Fellow
    thou, awake!

Varro

  My lord?

Claudius

  My lord?

Brutus

  Why did you so cry out, sirs, in your sleep?   305

Both

  Did we, my lord?

Brutus
                    Ay. Saw you any thing?

Varro
    No, my lord, I saw nothing.

Claudius
                        Nor I, my lord.

Brutus
    Go and commend me to my brother Cassius;
    Bid him set on his pow'rs betimes before,
    And we will follow.

Varro and Claudius
310   It shall be done, my lord.

                    [Exeunt.]

ACT FIVE

Scene I

Near Philippi.

[Enter OCTAVIUS, ANTONY, and their Army.]

Octavius
Now, Antony, our hopes are answered.
You said the enemy would not come down,
But keep the hills and upper regions;
It proves not so. Their battles are at hand;
They mean to warn us at Philippi here,   5
Answering before we do demand of them.

Antony
Tut, I am in their bosoms, and I know
Wherefore they do it. They could be content
To visit other places, and come down
With fearful bravery, thinking by this face   10
To fasten in our thoughts that they have courage;
But 'tis not so.

[Enter a Messenger.]

Messenger
                    Prepare you, generals:
The enemy comes on in gallant show;
Their bloody sign of battle is hung out,
And something to be done immediately.   15

Antony
Octavius, lead your battle softly on,
Upon the left hand of the even field.

Octavius
Upon the right hand I: keep thou the left.

Antony
Why do you cross me in this exigent?

Octavius
20   I do not cross you; but I will do so.

                [March.]

      [Drum. Enter BRUTUS, CASSIUS, *and their Army;*
        LUCILIUS, TITINIUS, MESSALA, *and Others.]*

Brutus
    They stand, and would have parley.
Cassius
    Stand fast, Titinius; we must out and talk.
Octavius
    Mark Antony, shall we give sign of battle?
Antony
    No, Caesar, we will answer on their charge.
25   Make forth; the generals would have some words.
Octavius
    Stir not until the signal.
Brutus
    Words before blows. Is it so, countrymen?
Octavius
    Not that we love words better, as you do.
Brutus
    Good words are better than bad strokes, Octavius.
Antony
30   In your bad strokes, Brutus, you give good words;
    Witness the hole you made in Caesar's heart,
    Crying 'Long live! Hail, Caesar!
Cassius
                        Antony,
    The posture of your blows are yet unknown;
    But for your words, they rob the Hybla bees,
    And leave them honeyless.
Antony
35   Not stingless too?
Brutus
    O yes, and soundless too;

For you have stol'n their buzzing, Antony,
And very wisely threat before you sting.

Antony

Villains, you did not so when your vile daggers
Hack'd one another in the sides of Caesar.   40
You show'd your teeth like apes, and fawn'd like
    hounds,
And bow'd like bondmen, kissing Caesar's feet;
Whilst damned Casca, like a cur, behind
Struck Caesar on the neck. O you flatterers!

Cassius

Flatterers! Now, Brutus, thank yourself: 45
This tongue had not offended so to-day
If Cassius might have rul'd.

Octavius

Come, come, the cause. If arguing make us sweat,
The proof of it will turn to redder drops.
Look,   50
I draw a sword against conspirators;
When think you that the sword goes up again?
Never till Caesar's three and thirty wounds
Be well aveng'd, or till another Caesar
Have added slaughter to the sword of traitors.   55

Brutus

Caesar, thou canst not die by traitors' hands,
Unless thou bring'st them with thee.

Octavius

                                        So I hope.
I was not born to die on Brutus' sword.

Brutus

O, if thou wert the noblest of thy strain,
Young man, thou couldst not die more honourable.   60

Cassius

A peevish schoolboy, worthless of such honour,
Join'd with a masker and a reveller!

Antony

Old Cassius still!

Octavius

              Come, Antony; away!
    Defiance, traitors, hurl we in your teeth.
65   If you dare fight to-day, come to the field;
    If not, when you have stomachs. *[Exeunt OCTAVIUS,*
        ANTONY, and their Army.]

Cassius

    Why, now, blow wind, swell billow, and swim bark!
    The storm is up, and all is on the hazard.

Brutus

    Ho, Lucilius! hark, a word with you.

Lucilius

    My lord.

       [BRUTUS and LUCILIUS converse apart.]

Cassius

    Messala.

Messala

             What says my general?

Cassius

70   Messala,
    This is my birth-day; as this very day
    Was Cassius born. Give me thy hand Messala.
    Be thou my witness that against my will,
    As Pompey was, am I compell'd to set
75   Upon one battle all our liberties.
    You know that I held Epicurus strong,
    And his opinion; now I change my mind,
    And partly credit things that do presage.
    Coming from Sardis, on our former ensign
80   Two mighty eagles fell; and there they perch'd,
    Gorging and feeding from our soldiers' hands,
    Who to Philippi here consorted us.
    This morning are they fled away and gone,
    And in their steads do ravens, crows, and kites,
85   Fly o'er our heads and downward look on us
    As we were sickly prey. Their shadows seem

A canopy most fatal, under which
Our army lies, ready to give up the ghost.

Messala

Believe not so.

Cassius

          I but believe it partly;
For I am fresh of spirit and resolv'd   90
To meet all perils very constantly.

Brutus

Even so, Lucilius.

Cassius

            Now, most noble Brutus,
The gods to-day stand friendly, that we may,
Lovers in peace, lead on our days to age!
But, since the affairs of men rest still in-certain,   95
Let's reason with the worst that may befall.
If we do lose this battle, then is this
The very last time we shall speak together.
What are you then determined to do?

Brutus

Even by the rule of that philosophy   100
By which I did blame Cato for the death
Which he did give himself – I know not how,
But I do find it cowardly and vile,
For fear of what might fall, so to prevent
The time of life – arming myself with patience   105
To stay the providence of some high powers
That govern us below.

Cassius

              Then, if we lose this battle,
You are contented to be led in triumph
Thorough the streets of Rome?

Brutus

No, Cassius, no. Think not, thou noble Roman,   110
That ever Brutus will go bound to Rome;
He bears too great a mind. But this same day
Must end that work the ides of March begun,

And whether we shall meet again I know not.
115   Therefore our everlasting farewell take:
For ever and for ever farewell, Cassius!
If we do meet again, why, we shall smile;
If not, why then this parting was well made.

Cassius

For ever and for ever farewell, Brutus!
120   If we do meet again, we'll smile indeed;
If not, 'tis true this parting was well made.

Brutus

Why then, lead on. O that a man might know
The end of this day's business ere it come!
But it sufficeth that the day will end,
125   And then the end is known. Come, ho! away!

[Exeunt.]

Scene II

Near Philippi. The field of battle.

[Alarum. Enter BRUTUS *and* MESSALA.*]*

Brutus
    Ride, ride, Messala, ride, and give these bills
    Unto the legions on the other side.

[Loud alarum.]

    Let them set on at once; for I perceive
    But cold demeanour in Octavius' wing,
    And sudden push gives them the overthrow.   5
    Ride, ride, Messala; let them all come down.

[Exeunt.]

Scene III

Another part of the field.

[Alarums. Enter CASSIUS and TITINIUS.]

Cassius

    O, look, Titinius, look, the villains fly!
    Myself have to mine own turn'd enemy.
    This ensign here of mine was turning back;
    I slew the coward, and did take it from him.

Titinius

5   O Cassius, Brutus gave the word too early,
    Who, having some advantage on Octavius,
    Took it too eagerly. His soldiers fell to spoil,
    Whilst we by Antony are all enclos'd.

[Enter PINDARUS.]

Pindarus

    Fly further off, my lord, fly further off;
10   Mark Antony is in your tents, my lord;
    Fly, therefore, noble Cassius, fly far off.

Cassius

    This hill is far enough. Look, look, Titinius.
    Are those my tents where I perceive the fire?

Titinius

    They are, my lord.

Cassius

                Titinius, if thou lovest me,
15   Mount thou my horse and hide thy spurs in him,
    Till he have brought thee up to yonder troops
    And here again, that I may rest assur'd
    Whether yond troops are friend or enemy.

Titinius

    I will be here again even with a thought. *[Exit.]*

Cassius

20   Go, Pindarus, get higher on that hill;
    My sight was ever thick; regard Titinius,

And tell me what thou not'st about the field.

[PINDARUS goes up.]

This day I breathed first. Time is come round,
And where I did begin there shall I end;
My life is run his compass. Sirrah, what news?   25
Pindarus
[Above] O my lord!
Cassius
What news?
Pindarus
Titinius is enclosed round about
With horsemen that make to him on the spur;
Yet he spurs on. Now they are almost on him.   30
Now Titinius! Now some light. O, he lights too!
He's ta'en. *[Shout.]*
And hark! They shout for joy.
Cassius
Come down; behold no more.
O, coward that I am to live so long   35
To see my best friend ta'en before my face!

[Enter PINDARUS.]

Come hither, sirrah.
In Parthia did I take thee prisoner;
And then I swore thee, saving of thy life,
That whatsoever I did bid thee do   40
Thou shouldst attempt it. Come now, keep thine oath;
Now be a freeman, and with this good sword,
That ran through Caesar's bowels, search this bosom.
Stand not to answer; here, take thou the hilts;
And when my face is cover'd, as 'tis now,   45
Guide thou the sword. *[PINDARUS stabs him.]*
                              Caesar, thou art reveng'd,
Even with the sword that kill'd thee. *[Dies.]*
Pindarus
So, I am free; yet would not so have been,

Durst I have done my will. O Cassius!
Far from this country Pindarus shall run,
50 Where never Roman shall take note of him.

[Exit.]

[Re-enter TITINIUS, *with* MESSALA.*]*

Messala
It is but change, Titinius; for Octavius
Is overthrown by noble Brutus' power,
As Cassius' legions are by Antony.
Titinius
55 These tidings will well comfort Cassius.
Messala
Where did you leave him?
Titinius
                                    All disconsolate,
With Pindarus, his bondman, on this hill.
Messala
Is not that he that lies upon the ground?
Titinius
He lies not like the living. O my heart!
Messala
Is not that he?
Titinius
60   No, this was he, Messala;
But Cassius is no more. O setting sun,
As in they red rays thou dost sink to night,
So in his red blood Cassius' day is set!
The sun of Rome is set. Our day is gone;
65 Clouds, dews, and dangers come; our deeds are done.
Mistrust of my success hath done this deed.
Messala
Mistrust of good success hath done this deed.
O hateful error, melancholy's child,
Why dost thou show to the apt thoughts of men
70 The things that are not? O error, soon conceiv'd,
Thou never com'st unto a happy birth,

But kill'st the mother that engend'red thee!
Titinius
What, Pindarus! Where art thou, Pindarus?
Messala
Seek him, Titinius, whilst I go to meet
The noble Brutus, thrusting this report   75
Into his ears. I may say 'thrusting' it;
For piercing steel and darts envenomed
Shall be as welcome to the ears of Brutus
As tidings of this sight.
Titinius
                Hie you, Messala,
And I will seek for Pindarus the while.   80

[Exit MESSALA.*]*

Why didst thou send me forth, brave Cassius?
Did I not meet they friends, and did not they
Put on my brows this wreath of victory,
And bid me give it thee? Didst thou not hear their
    shouts?
Alas, thou hast misconstrued every thing!   85
But hold thee, take this garland on thy brow;
Thy Brutus bid me give it thee, and I
Will do his bidding. Brutus, come apace,
And see how I regarded Caius Cassius.
By your leave, gods. This is a Roman's part.   90
Come, Cassius' sword, and find Titinius' heart.

[Dies.]

[Alarum. Re-enter MESSALA, *with* BRUTUS, YOUNG
CATO, STRATO, VOLUMNIUS, *and* LUCILIUS.*]*

Brutus
Where, where, Messala, doth his body lie?

Messala
 Lo yonder, and Titinius mourning it.
Brutus
 Titinius' face is upward.
Cato
        He is slain.
Brutus
95 O Julius Caesar, thou art mighty yet!
 Thy spirit walks abroad and turns our swords
 In our own proper entrails. *[Low alarums.]*
Cato
        Brave Titinius!
 Look whe'r he have not crown'd dead Cassius!
Brutus
 Are yet two Romans living such as these?
100 The last of all the Romans, fare thee well!
 It is impossible that ever Rome
 Should breed they fellow. Friends, I owe moe tears
 To this dead man than you shall see me pay.
 I shall find time, Cassius, I shall find time.
105 Come, therefore, and to Thasos send his body.
 His funerals shall not be in our camp,
 Lest it discomfort us. Lucilius, come;
 And come, young Cato; let us to the field.
 Labeo and Flavious set our battles on.
110 'Tis three o'clock; and, Romans, yet ere night
 We shall try fortune in a second fight.

[Exeunt.]

Scene IV

Another part of the field.

[Alarum. Enter BRUTUS, MESSALA, YOUNG CATO,
LUCILIUS, and FLAVIUS.]

Brutus
    Yet, countrymen, O, yet hold up your heads!
Cato
    What bastard doth not? Who will go with me?
    I will proclaim my name about the field:
    I am the son of Marcus Cato, ho!
    A foe to tyrants, and my country's friend.   5
    I am the son of Marcus Cato, ho!

[Enter Soldiers and fight.]

Brutus
    And I am Brutus, Marcus Brutus, I!
    Brutus, my country's friend! Know me for
    Brutus! *[Exit. YOUNG CATO falls.]*
Lucilius
    O young and noble Cato, art thou down?   10
    Why, now thou diest as bravely as Titinius,
    And mayst be honour'd, being Cato's son.
1 Soldier
    Yield, or thou diest.
Lucilius
               Only I yield to die.

[Offering money]

    There is so much that thou wilt kill me straight.
    Kill Brutus, and be honour'd in his death.
1 Soldier
    We must not. A noble prisoner!   15

[Enter ANTONY.]

2 Soldier
    Room, ho! Tell Antony Brutus is ta'en.
1 Soldier
    I'll tell the news. Here comes the general.
    Brutus is ta'en! Brutus is ta'en, my lord!
Antony
    Where is he?
Lucilius
20 Safe, Antony; Brutus is safe enough.
    I dare assure thee that no enemy
    Shall ever take alive the noble Brutus.
    The gods defend him from so great a shame!
    When you do find him, or alive or dead,
25 He will be found like Brutus, like himself.
Antony
    This is not Brutus, friend; but, I assure you,
    A prize no less in worth. Keep this man safe;
    Give him all kindness. I had rather have
    Such men my friends than enemies. Go on,
30 And see whe'r Brutus be alive or dead;
    And bring us word unto Octavius' tent
    How everything is chanc'd.

                    [Exeunt.]

Scene V

Another part of the field.

[Enter BRUTUS, DARDANIUS, CLITUS, STRATO, *and* VOLUMNIUS.*]*

Brutus
 Come, poor remains of friends, rest on this rock.
Clitus
 Statilius show'd the torch-light; but, my lord,
 He came not back. He is or ta'en or slain.
Brutus
 Sit thee down, Clitus. Slaying is the word;
 It is a deed in fashion. Hark thee, Clitus.   5

[Whispering.]

Clitus
 What, I, my lord? No, not for all the world.
Brutus
 Peace, then, no words.
Clitus
                          I'll rather kill myself.
Brutus
 Hark thee, Dardanius!
Dardanius
                          Shall I do such a deed?
Clitus
 O Dardanius!
Dardanius
 O Clitus!   10
Clitus
 What ill request did Brutus make to thee?
Dardanius
 To kill him, Clitus. Look, he meditates.
Clitus
 Now is that noble vessel full of grief,
 That it runs over even at his eyes.

Brutus

15 Come hither, good Volumnius; list a word.

Volumnius

What says my lord?

Brutus

                    Why, this, Volumnius:
The ghost of Caesar hath appear'd to me
Two several times by night – at Sardis once,
And this last night here in Philippi fields.
I know my hour is come.

Volumnius

20   Not so, my lord.

Brutus

Nay, I am sure it is, Volumnius.
Thou seest the world, Volumnius, how it goes:
Our enemies have beat us to the pit;

[Low alarums.]

It is more worthy to leap in ourselves
25 Than tarry till they push us. Good Volumnius,
Thou know'st that we two went to school together;
Even for that our love of old, I prithee,
Hold thou my sword-hilts whilst I run on it.

Volumnius

That's not an office for a friend, my lord. *[Alarum still.]*

Clitus

30 Fly, fly, my lord; there is no tarrying here.

Brutus

Farewell to you; and you; and you, Volumnius.
Strato, thou hast been all this while asleep;
Farewell to thee too, Strato. Countrymen,
My heart doth joy that yet in all my life
35 I found no man but he was true to me.
I shall have glory by this losing day,
More than Octavius and Mark Antony
By this vile conquest shall attain unto.
So fare you well at once; for Brutus' tongue

Hath almost ended his life's history.   40
Night hangs upon mine eyes; my bones would rest,
That have but labour'd to attain this hour.

[Alarum. Cry within 'Fly, fly, fly!']

Clitus
Fly, my lord, fly.
Brutus
                    Hence! I will follow.

[Exeunt CLITUS, DARDANIUS, and VOLUMNIUS.]

I prithee, Strato, stay thou by thy lord;
Thou art a fellow of a good respect;   45
Thy life hath had some smatch of honour in it.
Hold then my sword, and turn away thy face,
While I do run upon it. Wilt thou, Strato?
Strato
Give me your hand first. Fare you well, my lord.
Brutus
Farewell, good Strato. Caesar, now be still.   50
I kill'd not thee with half so good a will.

[He runs on his sword, and dies.]

*[Alarum. Retreat. Enter OCTAVIUS, ANTONY, MESSALA,
LUCILIUS, and the Army.]*

Octavius
What man is that?
Messala
My master's man. Strato, where is thy master?
Strato
Free from the bondage you are in, Messala.
The conquerors can but make a fire of him;   55
For Brutus only overcame himself,
And no man else hath honour by his death.

Lucilius
>So Brutus should be found. I thank thee, Brutus,
>That thou hast prov'd Lucilius' saying true.

Octavius
>60 All that serv'd Brutus, I will entertain them.
>Fellow, wilt thou bestow thy time with me?

Strato
>Ay, if Messala will prefer me to you.

Octavius
>Do so, good Messala.

Messala
>How died my master, Strato?

Strato
>65 I held the sword, and he did run on it.

Messala
>Octavius, then take him to follow thee,
>That did the latest service to my master.

Antony
>This was the noblest Roman of them all.
>All the conspirators save only he
>70 Did that they did in envy of great Caesar;
>He only in a general honest thought
>And common good to all made one of them.
>His life was gentle; and the elements
>So mix'd in him that Nature might stand up
>75 And say to all the world 'This was a man!'

Octavius
>According to his virtue let us use him,
>With all respect and rites of burial.
>Within my tent his bones to-night shall lie,
>Most like a soldier, ordered honourably.
>80 So call the field to rest, and let's away
>To part the glories of this happy day.

[Exeunt.]

Shakespeare: Words and Phrases

adapted from the Collins English Dictionary

abate 1 VERB to abate here means to lessen or diminish ❑ *There lives within the very flame of love/A kind of wick or snuff that will abate it* (*Hamlet 4.7*) 2 VERB to abate here means to shorten ❑ *Abate thy hours* (*A Midsummer Night's Dream 3.2*) 3 VERB to abate here means to deprive ❑ *She hath abated me of half my train* (*King Lear 2.4*)

abjure VERB to abjure means to renounce or give up ❑ *this rough magic I here abjure* (*Tempest 5.1*)

abroad ADV abroad means elsewhere or everywhere ❑ *You have heard of the news abroad* (*King Lear 2.1*)

abrogate VERB to abrogate means to put an end to ❑ *so it shall praise you to abrogate scurrility* (*Love's Labours Lost 4.2*)

abuse 1 NOUN abuse in this context means deception or fraud ❑ *What should this mean? Are all the rest come back?/ Or is it some abuse, and no such thing?* (*Hamlet 4.7*) 2 NOUN an abuse in this context means insult or offence ❑ *I will be deaf to pleading and excuses/ Nor tears nor prayers shall purchase our abuses* (*Romeo and Juliet 3.1*) 3 NOUN an abuse in this context means using something improperly ❑ *we'll digest/ Th'abuse*

of distance (*Henry II Chorus*) 4 NOUN an abuse in this context means doing something which is corrupt or dishonest ❑ *Come, bring them away: if these be good people in a commonweal that do nothing but their abuses in common houses, I know no law: bring them away.* (*Measure for Measure 2.1*)

abuser NOUN the abuser here is someone who betrays, a betrayer ❑ *I … do attach thee/ For an abuser of the world* (*Othello 1.2*)

accent NOUN accent here means language ❑ *In states unborn, and accents yet unknown* (*Julius Caesar 3.1*)

accident NOUN an accident in this context is an event or something that happened ❑ *think no more of this night's accidents* (*A Midsummer Night's Dream 4.1*)

accommodate VERB to accommodate in this context means to equip or to give someone the equipment to do something ❑ *The safer sense will ne'er accommodate/ His master thus.* (*King Lear 4.6*)

according ADJ according means sympathetic or ready to agree ❑ *within the scope of choice/ Lies* *my consent and fair according voice* (*Romeo and Juliet 1.2*)

account NOUN account often means judgement (by God) or reckoning ❏ *No reckoning made, but sent to my account/ With all my imperfections on my head* (*Hamlet 1.5*)

accountant ADJ accountant here means answerable or accountable ❏ *his offence is… /Accountant to the law* (*Measure for Measure 2.4*)

ace NOUN ace here means one or first referring to the lowest score on a dice ❏ *No die, but an ace, for him; for he is but one./ Less than an ace, man; for he is dead; he is nothing.* (*A Midsummer Night's Dream 5.1*)

acquit VERB here acquit means to be rid of or free of. It is related to the verb quit ❏ *I am glad I am so acquit of this tinderbox* (*The Merry Wives of Windsor 1.3*)

afeard ADJ afeard means afraid or frightened ❏ *Nothing afeard of what thyself didst make* (*Macbeth 1.3*)

affiance NOUN affiance means confidence or trust ❏ *O how hast thou with jealousy infected/ The sweetness of affiance* (*Henry V 2.2*)

affinity NOUN in this context, affinity means important connections, or relationships with important people ❏ *The Moor replies/ That he you hurt is of great fame in Cyprus,/ And great affinity* (*Othello 3.1*)

agnize VERB to agnize is an old word that means that you recognize or acknowledge something ❏ *I do agnize/ A natural and prompt alacrity I find in hardness* (*Othello 1.3*)

ague NOUN an ague is a fever in which the patient has hot and cold

shivers one after the other ❏ *This is some monster of the isle with four legs, who hath got … an ague* (*The Tempest 2.2*)

alarm, alarum NOUN an alarm or alarum is a call to arms or a signal for soldiers to prepare to fight ❏ *Whence cometh this alarum and the noise?* (*Henry VI part I 1.4*)

Albion NOUN Albion is another word for England ❏ *but I will sell my dukedom,/ To buy a slobbery and a dirty farm In that nook-shotten isle of Albion* (*Henry V 3.5*)

all of all PHRASE all of all means everything, or the sum of all things ❏ *The very all of all* (*Love's Labours Lost 5.1*)

amend VERB amend in this context means to get better or to heal ❏ *at his touch… They presently amend* (*Macbeth 4.3*)

anchor VERB if you anchor on something you concentrate on it or fix on it ❏ *My invention … Anchors on Isabel* (*Measure for Measure 2.4*)

anon ADV anon was a common word for soon ❏ *You shall see anon how the murderer gets the love of Gonzago's wife* (*Hamlet 3.2*)

antic 1 ADJ antic here means weird or strange ❏ *I'll charm the air to give a sound/ While you perform your antic round* (*Macbeth 4.1*) 2 NOUN in this context antic means a clown or a strange, unattractive creature ❏ *If black, why nature, drawing an antic,/ Made a foul blot* (*Much Ado About Nothing 3.1*)

apace ADV apace was a common word for quickly ❏ *Come apace* (*As You Like It 3.3*)

apparel NOUN apparel means clothes or clothing ❏ *one suit of apparel* (*Hamlet 3.2*)

appliance NOUN appliance here means cure ❏ *Diseases desperate grown/ By desperate appliance are relieved* (*Hamlet 4.3*)

argument NOUN argument here means a topic of conversation or the subject ❏ *Why 'tis the rarest argument of wonder that hath shot out in our latter times* (*All's Well That Ends Well 2.3*)

arrant ADJ arrant means absolute, complete. It strengthens the meaning of a noun ❏ *Fortune, that arrant whore* (*King Lear 2.4*)

arras NOUN an arras is a tapestry, a large cloth with a picture sewn on it using coloured thread ❏ *Behind the arras I'll convey myself/ To hear the process* (*Hamlet 3.3*)

art 1 NOUN art in this context means knowledge ❏ *Their malady convinces/ The great essay of art* (*Macbeth 4.3*) 2 NOUN art can also mean skill as it does here ❏ *He ... gave you such a masterly report/ For art and exercise in your defence* (*Hamlet 4.7*) 3 NOUN art here means magic ❏ *Now I want/ Spirits to enforce, art to enchant* (*The Tempest 5 Epilogue*)

assay 1 NOUN an assay was an attempt, a try ❏ *Make assay./ Bow, stubborn knees* (*Hamlet 3.3*) 2 NOUN assay can also mean a test or a trial ❏ *he hath made assay of her virtue* (*Measure for Measure 3.1*)

attend (on/upon) VERB attend on means to wait for or to expect ❏ *Tarry I here, I but attend on death* (*Two Gentlemen of Verona 3.1*)

auditor NOUN an auditor was a member of an audience or someone who listens ❏ *I'll be an auditor* (*A Midsummer Night's Dream 3.1*)

aught NOUN aught was a common word which meant anything ❏ *if my love thou holdest at aught* (*Hamlet 4.3*)

aunt 1 NOUN an aunt was another word for an old woman and also means someone who talks a lot or a gossip ❏ *The wisest aunt telling the saddest tale* (*A Midsummer Night's Dream 2.1*) 2 NOUN aunt could also mean a mistress or a prostitute ❏ *the thrush and the jay/ Are summer songs for me and my aunts/ While we lie tumbling in the hay* (*The Winter's Tale 4.3*)

avaunt EXCLAM avaunt was a common word which meant go away ❏ *Avaunt, you curs!* (*King Lear 3.6*)

aye ADV here aye means always or ever ❏ *Whose state and honour I for aye allow* (*Richard II 5.2*)

baffle VERB baffle meant to be disgraced in public or humiliated ❏ *I am disgraced, impeached, and baffled here* (*Richard II 1.1*)

bald ADJ bald means trivial or silly ❏ *I knew 'twould be a bald conclusion* (*The Comedy of Errors 2.2*)

ban NOUN a ban was a curse or an evil spell ❏ *Sometimes with lunatic bans... Enforce their charity* (*King Lear 2.3*)

barren ADJ barren meant empty or hollow ❏ *now I let go your hand, I am barren.* (*Twelfth Night 1.3*)

base ADJ base is an adjective that means unworthy or dishonourable ❏ *civet is of a baser birth than tar* (*As You Like It 3.2*)

base 1 ADJ base can also mean of low social standing or someone who was not part of the ruling class ❏ *Why brand they us with 'base'?* (*King Lear* 1.2) 2 ADJ here base means poor quality ❏ *Base cousin,/ Darest thou break first?* (*Two Noble Kinsmen* 3.3)

bawdy NOUN bawdy means obscene or rude ❏ *Bloody, bawdy villain!* (*Hamlet* 2.2)

bear in hand PHRASE bear in hand means taken advantage of or fooled ❏ *This I made good to you In our last conference, passed in probation with you/How you were borne in hand* (*Macbeth* 3.1)

beard VERB to beard someone was to oppose or confront them ❏ *Com'st thou to beard me in Denmark?* (*Hamlet* 2.2)

beard, in one's PHRASE if you say something in someone's beard you say it to their face ❏ *I will verify as much in his beard* (*Henry V* 3.2)

beaver NOUN a beaver was a visor on a battle helmet ❏ *O yes, my lord, he wore his beaver up* (*Hamlet* 1.2)

become VERB if something becomes you it suits you or is appropriate to you ❏ *Nothing in his life became him like the leaving it* (*Macbeth* 1.4)

bed, brought to PHRASE to be brought to bed means to give birth ❏ *His wife but yesternight was brought to bed* (*Titus Andronicus* 4.2)

bedabbled ADJ if something is bedabbled it is sprinkled ❏ *Bedabbled with the dew, and torn with briers* (*A Midsummer Night's Dream* 3.2)

Bedlam NOUN Bedlam was a word used for Bethlehem Hospital which was a place the insane were sent to ❏ *The country give me proof and precedent/Of Bedlam beggars* (*King Lear* 2.3)

bed-swerver NOUN a bed-swerver was someone who was unfaithful in marriage, an adulterer ❏ *she's/A bed-swerver* (*Winter's Tale* 2.1)

befall 1 VERB to befall is to happen, occur or take place ❏ *In this same interlude it doth befall/That I present a wall* (*A Midsummer Night's Dream* 5.1) 2 VERB to befall can also mean to happen to someone or something ❏ *fair befall thee and thy noble house* (*Richard III* 1.3)

behoof NOUN behoof was an advantage or benefit ❏ *All our surgeons/Convent in their behoof* (*Two Noble Kinsmen* 1.4)

beldam NOUN a beldam was a witch or old woman ❏ *Have I not reason, beldams as you are?* (*Macbeth* 3.5)

belike ADV belike meant probably, perhaps or presumably ❏ *belike he likes it not* (*Hamlet* 3.2)

bent 1 NOUN bent means a preference or a direction ❏ *Let me work,/For I can give his humour true bent,/And I will bring him to the Capitol* (*Julius Caesar* 2.1) 2 ADJ if you are bent on something you are determined to do it ❏ *for now I am bent to know/By the worst means the worst.* (*Macbeth* 3.4)

beshrew VERB beshrew meant to curse or wish evil on someone ❏ *much beshrew my manners and my pride/If Hermia meant to say Lysander lied* (*A Midsummer Night's Dream* 2.2)

betime (s) ADV betime means early ❏ *To business that we love we rise betime* (*Antony and Cleopatra* 4.4)

bevy NOUN bevy meant type or sort, it was also used to mean company ❏ *many more of the same bevy* (*Hamlet* 5.2)

blazon VERB to blazon something meant to display or show it ❏ *that thy skill be more to blazon it* (*Romeo and Juliet* 2.6)

blind ADJ if you are blind when you do something you are reckless or do not care about the consequences ❏ *are you yet to your own souls so blind/ That two you will war with God by murdering me* (*Richard III* 1.4)

bombast NOUN bombast was wool stuffing (used in a cushion for example) and so it came to mean padded out or long-winded. Here it means someone who talks a lot about nothing in particular ❏ *How now my sweet creature of bombast* (*Henry IV part I* 2.4)

bond 1 NOUN a bond is a contract or legal deed ❏ *Well, then, your bond, and let me see* (*Merchant of Venice* 1.3) 2 NOUN bond could also mean duty or commitment ❏ *I love your majesty/ According to my bond* (*King Lear* 1.1)

bottom NOUN here bottom means essence, main point or intent ❏ *Now I see/ The bottom of your purpose* (*All's Well That Ends Well* 3.7)

bounteously ADV bounteously means plentifully, abundantly ❏ *I prithee, and I'll pay thee bounteously* (*Twelfth Night* 1.2)

brace 1 NOUN a brace is a couple or two ❏ *Have lost a brace of kinsmen* (*Romeo and Juliet* 5.3) 2 NOUN if you are in a brace position it means you are ready ❏ *For that it stands not in such warlike brace* (*Othello* 1.3)

brand VERB to mark permanantly like the markings on cattle ❏ *the wheeled seat/ Of fortunate Caesar ... branded his baseness that ensued* (*Anthony and Cleopatra* 4.14)

brave ADJ brave meant fine, excellent or splendid ❏ *O brave new world/ That has such people in't* (*The Tempest* 5.1)

brine NOUN brine is sea-water ❏ *He shall drink nought brine, for I'll not show him/ Where the quick freshes are* (*The Tempest* 3.2)

brow NOUN brow in this context means appearance ❏ *doth hourly grow/ Out of his brows* (*Hamlet* 3.3)

burden 1 NOUN the burden here is a chorus ❏ *I would sing my song without a burden* (*As You Like It* 3.2) 2 NOUN burden means load or weight (this is the current meaning) ❏ *the scarfs and the bannerets about thee did manifoldly dissuade me from believing thee a vessel of too great a burden* (*All's Well that Ends Well* 2.3)

buttons, in one's PHRASE this is a phrase that means clear, easy to see ❏ *Tis in his buttons he will carry't* (*The Merry Wives of Windsor* 3.2)

cable NOUN cable here means scope or reach ❏ *The law ... Will give her cable* (*Othello* 1.2)

cadent ADJ if something is cadent it is falling or dropping ❏ *With cadent tears fret channels in her cheeks* (*King Lear* 1.4)

canker VERB to canker is to decay, become corrupt ❏ *And, as with age his body uglier grows,/ So his mind cankers* (*The Tempest 4.1*)

canon, from the PHRASE from the canon is an expression meaning out of order, improper ❏ *Twas from the canon* (*Coriolanus 3.1*)

cap-a-pie ADV cap-a-pie means from head to foot, completely ❏ *I am courtier cap-a-pie* (*The Winter's Tale 4.4*)

carbonadoed ADJ if something is carbonadoed it is cut or scored (scratched) with a knife ❏ *it is your carbonadoed* (*All's Well That Ends Well 4.5*)

carouse VERB to carouse is to drink at length, party ❏ *They cast their caps up and carouse together* (*Anthony and Cleopatra 4.12*)

carrack NOUN a carrack was a large old ship, a galleon ❏ *Faith, he tonight hath boarded a land-carrack* (*Othello 1.2*)

cassock NOUN a cassock here means a military cloak, long coat ❏ *half of the which dare not shake the snow from off their cassocks lest they shake themselves to pieces* (*All's Well That Ends Well 4.3*)

catastrophe NOUN catastrophe here means conclusion or end ❏ *pat he comes, like the catastrophe of the old comedy* (*King Lear 1.2*)

cautel NOUN a cautel was a trick or a deceptive act ❏ *Perhaps he loves you now/ And now no soil not cautel doth besmirch* (*Hamlet 1.2*)

celerity NOUN celerity was a common word for speed, swiftness ❏ *Hence hath offence his quick celerity/ When it is borne in high authority* (*Measure for Measure 4.2*)

chafe NOUN chafe meant anger or temper ❏ *this Herculean Roman does become/ The carriage of his chafe* (*Anthony and Cleopatra 1.3*)

chanson NOUN chanson was an old word for a song ❏ *The first row of the pious chanson will show you more* (*Hamlet 2.2*)

chapman NOUN a chapman was a trader or merchant ❏ *Not uttered by base sale of chapman's tongues* (*Love's Labours Lost 2.1*)

chaps, chops NOUN chaps (and chops) was a word for jaws ❏ *Which ne'er shook hands nor bade farewell to him/ Till he unseamed him from the nave to th' chops* (*Macbeth 1.2*)

chattels NOUN chattels were your moveable possessions. The word is used in the traditional marriage ceremony ❏ *She is my goods, my chattels* (*The Taming of the Shrew 3.3*)

chide VERB if you are chided by someone you are told off or reprimanded ❏ *Now I but chide, but I should use thee worse* (*A Midsummer Night's Dream 3.2*)

chinks NOUN chinks was a word for cash or money ❏ *he that can lay hold of her/ Shall have the chinks* (*Romeo and Juliet 1.5*)

choleric ADJ if something was called choleric it meant that they were quick to get angry ❏ *therewithal unruly waywardness that infirm and choleric years bring with them* (*King Lear 1.1*)

chuff NOUN a chuff was a miser,

someone who clings to his or her money ❑ *ye fat chuffs* (*Henry IV part I 2.2*)

cipher NOUN cipher here means nothing ❑ *Mine were the very cipher of a function* (*Measure for Measure 2.2*)

circummured ADJ circummured means that something is surrounded with a wall ❑ *He hath a garden circummured with brick* (*Measure for Measure 4.1*)

civet NOUN a civet is a type of scent or perfume ❑ *Give me an ounce of civet* (*King Lear 4.6*)

clamorous ADJ clamorous means noisy or boisterous ❑ *Be clamorous and leap all civil bounds* (*Twelfth Night 1.4*)

clangour, clangor NOUN clangour is a word that means ringing (the sound that bells make) ❑ *Like to a dismal clangour heard from far* (*Henry VI part III 2.3*)

cleave VERB if you cleave to something you stick to it or are faithful to it ❑ *Thy thoughts I cleave to* (*The Tempest 4.1*)

clock and clock, 'twixt PHRASE from hour to hour, without stopping or continuously ❑ *To weep 'twixt clock and clock* (*Cymbeline 3.4*)

close ADJ here close means hidden ❑ *Stand close; this is the same Athenian* (*A Midsummer Night's Dream 3.2*)

cloud NOUN a cloud on your face means that you have a troubled, unhappy expression ❑ *He has cloud in's face* (*Anthony and Cleopatra 3.2*)

cloy VERB if you cloy an appetite you satisfy it ❑ *Other women cloy/The appetites they feed* (*Anthony and Cleopatra 2.2*)

cock-a-hoop, set PHRASE if you set cock-a-hoop you become free of everything ❑ *You will set cock-a-hoop* (*Romeo and Juliet 1.5*)

colours NOUN colours is a word used to describe battle-flags or banners. Sometimes we still say that we nail our colours to the mast if we are stating which team or side of an argument we support ❑ *the approbation of those that weep this lamentable divorce under her colours* (*Cymbeline 1.5*)

combustion NOUN combustion was a word meaning disorder or chaos ❑ *prophesying ... Of dire combustion and confused events* (*Macbeth 2.3*)

comely ADJ if you are or something is comely you or it is lovely, beautiful, graceful ❑ *O, what a world is this, when what is comely/Envenoms him that bears it!* (*As You Like It 2.3*)

commend VERB if you commend yourself to someone you send greetings to them ❑ *Commend me to my brother* (*Measure for Measure 1.4*)

compact NOUN a compact is an agreement or a contract ❑ *what compact mean you to have with us?* (*Julius Caesar 3.1*)

compass 1 NOUN here compass means range or scope ❑ *you would sound me from my lowest note to the top of my compass* (*Hamlet 3.2*) 2 VERB to compass here means to achieve, bring about or make happen ❑ *How now shall this be compassed?/Canst thou bring me to the party?* (*Tempest 3.2*)

comptible ADJ comptible is an old word meaning sensitive ❏ *I am very comptible, even to the least sinister usage.* (*Twelfth Night 1.5*)

confederacy NOUN a confederacy is a group of people usually joined together to commit a crime. It is another word for a conspiracy ❏ *Lo, she is one of this confederacy!* (*A Midsummer Night's Dream 3.2*)

confound VERB if you confound something you confuse it or mix it up; it also means to stop or prevent ❏ *A million fail, confounding oath on oath.* (*A Midsummer Night's Dream 3.2*)

contagion NOUN contagion is an old word for disease or poison ❏ *hell itself breathes out/Contagion to this world* (*Hamlet 3.2*)

contumely NOUN contumely is an old word for an insult ❏ *the proud man's contumely* (*Hamlet 3.1*)

counterfeit 1 VERB if you counterfeit something you copy or imitate it ❏ *Meantime your cheeks do counterfeit our roses* (*Henry VI part I 2.4*) 2 VERB in this context counterfeit means to pretend or make believe ❏ *I will counterfeit the bewitchment of some popular man* (*Coriolanus*)

coz NOUN coz was a shortened form of the word cousin ❏ *sweet my coz, be merry* (*As You Like It 1.2*)

cozenage NOUN cozenage is an old word meaning cheating or a deception ❏ *Thrown out his angle for my proper life,/And with such coz'nage* (*Hamlet 5.2*)

crave VERB crave used to mean to beg or request ❏ *I crave your pardon* (*The Comedy of Errors 1.2*)

crotchet NOUN crotchets are strange ideas or whims ❏ *thou hast some strange crotchets in thy head now* (*The Merry Wives of Windsor 2.1*)

cuckold NOUN a cuckold is a man whose wife has been unfaithful to him ❏ *As there is no true cuckold but calamity* (*Twelfth Night 1.5*)

cuffs, go to PHRASE this phrase meant to fight ❏ *the player went to cuffs in the question* (*Hamlet 2.2*)

cup VERB in this context cup is a verb which means to pour drink or fill glasses with alcohol ❏ *cup us til the world go round* (*Anthony and Cleopatra 2.7*)

cur NOUN cur is an insult meaning dog and is also used to mean coward ❏ *Out, dog! out, cur! Thou drivest me past the bounds/Of maiden's patience* (*A Midsummer Night's Dream 3.2*)

curiously ADV in this context curiously means carefully or skilfully ❏ *The sleeves curiously cut* (*The Taming of the Shrew 4.3*)

curry VERB curry means to flatter or to praise someone more than they are worth ❏ *I would curry with Master Shallow that no man could better command his servants* (*Henry IV part II 5.1*)

custom NOUN custom is a habit or a usual practice ❏ *Hath not old custom made this life more sweet/Than that of painted pomp?* (*As You Like It 2.1*)

cutpurse NOUN a cutpurse is an old word for a thief. Men used to carry their money in small bags (purse) that hung from their belts; thieves would cut the purse from the belt and steal their money ❏ *A cutpurse of the empire and the rule* (*Hamlet 3.4*)

dainty ADJ dainty used to mean splendid, fine ❑ *Why, that's my dainty Ariel!* (*Tempest 5.1*)

dally VERB if you dally with something you play with it or tease it ❑ *They that dally nicely with words may quickly make them wanton* (*Twelfth Night 3.1*)

damask COLOUR damask is a light-red or pink colour ❑ *Twas just the difference/ Betwixt the constant red and mingled damask* (*As You Like It 3.5*)

dare 1 VERB dare means to challeng or, confront ❑ *He goes before me, and still dares me on* (*A Midsummer Night's Dream 3.3*) 2 VERB dare in this context means to present, deliver or inflict ❑ *all that fortune, death, and danger dare* (*Hamlet 4.4*)

darkly ADV darkly was used in this context to mean secretly or cunningly ❑ *I will go darkly to work with her* (*Measure for Measure 5.1*)

daw NOUN a daw was a slang term for idiot or fool (after the bird jackdaw which was famous for its stupidity) ❑ *Yea, just so much as you may take upon a knife's point and choke a daw withal* (*Much Ado About Nothing 3.1*)

debile ADJ debile meant weak or feeble ❑ *And debile minister great power* (*All's Well That Ends Well 2.3*)

deboshed ADJ deboshed was another way of saying corrupted or debauched ❑ *Men so disordered, deboshed and bold* (*King Lear 1.4*)

decoct VERB to decoct was to heat up, warm something ❑ *Can sodden water,/ A drench for sur-reained jades*

... Decoct their cold blood to such valiant heat? (*Henry V 3.5*)

deep-revolving ADJ deep-revolving here uses the idea that you turn something over in your mind when you are thinking hard about it and so means deep-thinking, meditating ❑ *The deep-revolving Buckingham/ No more shall be the neighbour to my counsels* (*Richard III 4.2*)

defect NOUN defect here means shortcoming or something that is not right ❑ *Being unprepared/ Our will became the servant to defect* (*Macbeth 2.1*)

degree 1 NOUN degree here means rank, standing or station ❑ *Should a like language use to all degrees,/ And mannerly distinguishment leave out/ Betwixt the prince and beggar* (*The Winter's Tale 2.1*) 2 NOUN in this context, degree means extent or measure ❑ *her offence/ Must be of such unnatural degree* (*King Lear 1.1*)

deify VERB if you deify something or someone you worship it or them as a God ❑ *all.. deifying the name of Rosalind* (*As You Like It 3.2*)

delated ADJ delated here means detailed ❑ *the scope/ Of these delated articles* (*Hamlet 1.2*)

delicate ADJ if something was described as delicate it meant it was of fine quality or valuable ❑ *thou wast a spirit too delicate* (*The Tempest 1.2*)

demise VERB in this context demise means to transmit, give or convey ❑ *what state ... Canst thou demise to any child of mine?* (*Richard III 4.4*)

deplore VERB to deplore means to express with grief or sorrow ❑ *Never more/ Will I my master's tears to you deplore* (*Twelfth Night 3.1*)

depose VERB if you depose someone you make them take an oath, or swear something to be true ❑ *Depose him in the justice of his cause* (*Richard II 1.3*)

depositary NOUN a depositary is a trustee ❑ *Made you ... my depositary* (*King Lear 2.4*)

derive 1 VERB to derive means to comes from or to descend (it usually applies to people) ❑ *No part of it is mine,/ This shame derives itself from unknown loins.* (*Much Ado About Nothing 4.1*) 2 VERB if you derive something from someone you inherit it ❑ *Treason is not inherited ...Or, if we derive it from our friends/ What's that to me?* (*As You Like It 1.3*)

descry VERB to see or catch sight of ❑ *The news is true, my lord. He is descried* (*Anthony and Cleopatra 3.7*)

desert 1 NOUN desert means worth or merit ❑ *That dost in vile misprison shackle up/ My love and her desert* (*All's Well That Ends Well 2.3*) 2 ADJ desert is used here to mean lonely or isolated ❑ *if that love or gold/ Can in this desert place buy entertainment* (*As You LIke It 2.4*)

design 1 VERB to design means to indicate or point out ❑ *we shall see/ Justice design the victor's chivalry* (*Richard II 1.1*) 2 NOUN a design is a plan, an intention or an undertaking ❑ *hinder not the honour of his design* (*All's Well That Ends Well 3.6*)

designment NOUN a designment was a plan or undertaking ❑ *The desperate tempest hath so bang'd the Turks,/ That their designment halts* (*Othello 2.1*)

despite VERB despite here means to spite or attempt to thwart a plan ❑ *Only to despite them I will endeavour anything* (*Much Ado About Nothing 2.2*)

device NOUN a device is a plan, plot or trick ❑ *Excellent, I smell a device* (*Twelfth Night 2.3*)

disable VERB to disable here means to devalue or make little of ❑ *he disabled my judgement* (*As You Like It 5.4*)

discandy VERB here discandy means to melt away or dissolve ❑ *The hearts ... do discandy , melt their sweets* (*Anthony and Cleopatra 4.12*)

disciple VERB to disciple is to teach or train ❑ *He ...was/ Discipled of the bravest* (*All's Well That Ends Well 1.2*)

discommend VERB if you discommend something you criticize it ❑ *my dialect which you discommend so much* (*King Lear 2.2*)

discourse NOUN discourse means conversation, talk or chat ❑ *which part of it I'll waste/ With such discourse as I not doubt shall make it/ Go quick away* (*The Tempest 5.1*)

discover VERB discover used to mean to reveal or show ❑ *the Prince discovered to Claudio that he loved my niece* (*Much Ado About Nothing 1.2*)

disliken VERB disguise, make unlike ❑ *disliken/ The truth of your own seeming* (*The Winter's Tale 4.4*)

dismantle VERB to dismantle is to remove or take away ❑ *Commit a thing so monstrous to dismantle/*

So many folds of favour (*King Lear 1.1*)

disponge VERB disponge means to pour out or rain down ❏ *The poisonous damp of night disponge upon me* (*Anthony and Cleopatra 4.9*)

distrain VERB to distrain something is to confiscate it ❏ *My father's goods are all distrained and sold* (*Richard II 2.3*)

divers ADJ divers is an old word for various ❏ *I will give out divers schedules of my beauty* (*Twelfth Night 1.5*)

doff VERB to doff is to get rid of or dispose ❏ *make our women fight/ To doff their dire distresses* (*Macbeth 4.3*)

dog VERB if you dog someone or something you follow them or it closely ❏ *I will rather leave to see Hector than not to dog him* (*Troilus and Cressida 5.1*)

dotage NOUN dotage here means infatuation ❏ *Her dotage now I do begin to pity* (*A Midsummer Night's Dream 4.1*)

dotard NOUN a dotard was an old fool ❏ *I speak not like a dotard nor a fool* (*Much Ado About Nothing 5.1*)

dote VERB to dote is to love, cherish, care without seeing any fault ❏ *And won her soul; and she, sweet lady, dotes,/ Devoutly dotes, dotes in idolatry* (*A Midsummer Night's Dream 1.1*)

doublet NOUN a doublet was a man's close-fitting jacket with short skirt ❏ *Lord Hamlet, with his doublet all unbraced* (*Hamlet 2.1*)

dowager NOUN a dowager is a widow ❏ *Like to a step-dame or a dowage* (*A Midsummer Night's Dream 1.1*)

dowdy NOUN a dowdy was an ugly woman ❏ *Dido was a dowdy* (*Romeo and Juliet 2.4*)

dower NOUN a dower (or dowery) is the riches or property given by the father of a bride to her husband-to-be ❏ *Thy truth then by they dower* (*King Lear 1.1*)

dram NOUN a dram is a tiny amount ❏ *Why, everything adheres together that no dram of a scruple* (*Twelfth Night 3.4*)

drift NOUN drift is a plan, scheme or intention ❏ *Shall Romeo by my letters know our drift* (*Romeo and Juliet 4.1*)

dropsied ADJ dropsied means pretentious ❏ *Where great additions swell's and virtues none/ It is a dropsied honour* (*All's Well That Ends Well 2.3*)

drudge NOUN a drudge was a slave, servant ❏ *If I be his cuckold, he's my drudge* (*All's Well That Ends Well 1.3*)

dwell VERB to dwell sometimes meant to exist, to be ❏ *I'd rather dwell in my necessity* (*Merchant of Venice 1.3*)

earnest ADJ an earnest was a pledge to pay or a payment in advance ❏ *for an earnest of a greater honour/ He bade me from him call thee Thane of Cawdor* (*Macbeth 1.3*)

ecstasy NOUN madness ❏ *This is the very ecstasy of love* (*Hamlet 2.1*)

edict NOUN law or declaration ❏ *It stands as an edict in destiny.* (*A Midsummer Night's Dream 1.1*)

egall ADJ egall is an old word meaning equal ❑ *companions/Whose souls do bear an egall yoke of love* (Merchant of Venice 2.4)

eisel NOUN eisel meant vinegar ❑ *Woo't drink up eisel?* (Hamlet 5.1)

eke, eke out VERB eke meant to add to, to increase. Eke out nowadays means to make something last as long as possible – particularly in the sense of making money last a long time ❑ *Still be kind/And eke out our performance with your mind* (Henry V Chorus)

elbow, out at PHRASE out at elbow is an old phrase meaning in poor condition – as when your jacket sleeves are worn at the elbow which shows that it is an old jacket ❑ *He cannot, sir. He's out at elbow* (Measure for Measure 2.1)

element NOUN elements were thought to be the things from which all things were made. They were: air, earth, water and fire ❑ *Does not our lives consist of the four elements?* (Twelfth Night 2.3)

elf VERB to elf was to tangle ❑ *I'll ... elf all my hairs in knots* (King Lear 2.3)

embassy NOUN an embassy was a message ❑ *We'll once more hear Orsino's embassy.* (Twelfth Night 1.5)

emphasis NOUN emphasis here means a forceful expression or strong statement ❑ *What is he whose grief/Bears such an emphasis* (Hamlet 5.1)

empiric NOUN an empiric was an untrained doctor sometimes called a quack ❑ *we must not ... prostitute our past-cure malady/To empirics* (All's Well That Ends Well 2.1)

emulate ADJ emulate here means envious ❑ *pricked on by a most emulate pride* (Hamlet 1.1)

enchant VERB to enchant meant to put a magic spell on ❑ *Damn'd as thou art, thou hast enchanted her,/For I'll refer me to all things of sense* (Othello 1.2)

enclog VERB to enclog was to hinder something or to provide an obstacle to it ❑ *Traitors enscarped to enclog the guitless keel* (Othello 1.2)

endure VERB to endure was to allow or to permit ❑ *and will endure/Our setting down before't.* (Macbeth 5.4)

enfranchise VERB if you enfranchised something you set it free ❑ *Do this or this;/Take in that kingdom and enfranchise that;/Perform't, or else we damn thee.'* (Anthony and Cleopatra 1.1)

engage VERB to engage here means to pledge or to promise ❑ *This to be true I do engage my life* (As You Like It 5.4)

engaol VERB to lock up or put in prison ❑ *Within my mouth you have engaoled my tongue* (Richard II 1.3)

engine NOUN an engine was a plot, device or a machine ❑ *their promises, enticements, oaths, tokens, and all these engines, of lust, are not the things they go under* (All's Well That Ends Well 3.5)

englut VERB if you were engulfed you were swallowed up or eaten whole ❑ *For certainly thou art so near the gulf,/Thou needs must be englutted.* (Henry V 4.3)

enjoined ADJ enjoined describes people joined together for the same reason ❑ *Of enjoined penitents/*

There's four or five (All's Well That Ends Well 3.5)

entertain 1 VERB to entertain here means to welcome or receive ❏ *Approach, rich Ceres, her to entertain. (The Tempest 4.1)* 2 VERB to entertain in this context means to cherish, hold in high regard or to respect ❏ *and I quake,/ Lest thou a feverous life shouldst entertain/ And six or seven winters more respect/ Than a perpetual honour. (Measure for Measure 3.1)* 3 VERB to entertain means here to give something consideration ❏ *But entertain it,/ And though you think me poor, I am the man/ Will give thee all the world. (Anthony and Cleopatra 2.7)* 4 VERB to entertain here means to treat or handle ❏ *your highness is not entertained with that ceremonious affection as you were wont (King Lear 1.4)*

envious ADJ envious meant spiteful or vindictive ❏ *he shall appear to the envious a scholar (Measure for Measure 3.2)*

ere PREP ere was a common word for before ❏ *ere this I should ha' fatted all the region kites (Hamlet 2.2)*

err VERB to err means to go astray, to make a mistake ❏ *And as he errs, doting on Hermia's eyes (A Midsummer Night's Dream 1.1)*

erst ADV erst was a common word for once or before ❏ *that erst brought sweetly forth/ The freckled cowslip (Henry V 5.2)*

eschew VERB if you eschew something you deliberately avoid doing it ❏ *What cannot be eschewed must be embraced (The Merry Wives of Windsor 5.5)*

escote VERB to escote meant to pay for, support ❏ *How are they escoted? (Hamlet 2.2)*

estimable ADJ estimable meant appreciative ❏ *I could not with such estimable wonder over-far believe that (Twelfth Night 2.1)*

extenuate VERB extenuate means to lessen ❏ *Which by no means we may extenuate (A Midsummer Night's Dream 1.1)*

fain ADV fain was a common word meaning gladly or willingly ❏ *I would fain prove so (Hamlet 2.2)*

fall NOUN in a voice or music fall meant going higher and lower ❏ *and so die/ That strain again! it had a dying fall (Twelfth Night 1.1)*

false ADJ false was a common word for treacherous ❏ *this is counter, you false Danish dogs! (Hamlet 4.5)*

fare VERB fare means to get on or manage ❏ *I fare well (The Taming of the Shrew Introduction 2)*

feign VERB to feign was to make up, pretend or fake ❏ *It is the more like to be feigned (Twelfth Night 1.5)*

fie EXCLAM fie was an exclamation of disgust ❏ *Fie, that you'll say so! (Twelfth Night 1.3)*

figure VERB to figure was to symbolize or look like ❏ *Wings and no eyes, figure unheedy haste (A Midsummer Night's Dream 1.1)*

filch VERB if you filch something you steal it ❏ *With cunning hast thou filch'd my daughter's heart (A Midsummer Night's Dream 1.1)*

flout VERB to flout something meant to scorn it ❏ *Why will you suffer her to flout me thus? (A Midsummer Night's Dream 3.2)*

fond ADJ fond was a common word meaning foolish ❏ *Shall we their fond pageant see?* (*A Midsummer Night's Dream 3.2*)

footing 1 NOUN footing meant landing on shore, arrival, disembarkation ❏ *Whose footing here anticipates our thoughts/ A se'nnight's speed.* (*Othello 2.1*) 2 NOUN footing also means support ❏ *there your charity would have lacked footing* (*Winter's Tale 3.3*)

forsooth ADV in truth, certainly, truly
❏ *I had rather, forsooth, go before you like a man* (*The Merry Wives of Windsor 3.2*)

forswear VERB if you forswear you lie, swear falsely or break your word ❏ *he swore a thing to me on Monday night, which he forswore on Tuesday morning* (*Much Ado About Nothing 5.1*)

freshes NOUN a fresh is a fresh water stream ❏ *He shall drink nought brine, for I'll not show him/ Where the quick freshes are.* (*Tempest 3.2*)

furlong NOUN a furlong is a measure of distance. It is the equivalent on one eight of a mile ❏ *Now would I give a thousand furlongs of sea for an acre of barren ground* (*Tempest 1.1*)

gaberdine NOUN a gaberdine is a cloak ❏ *My best way is to creep under his gaberdine* (*Tempest 2.2*)

gage NOUN a gage was a challenge to duel or fight ❏ *There is my gage, Aumerle, in gage to thine* (*Richard II 4.1*)

gait NOUN your gait is your way of walking or step ❏ *I know her by her gait* (*Tempest 4.1*)

gall VERB to gall is to annoy or irritate ❏ *Let it not gall your patience, good Iago,/ That I extend my manners* (*Othello 2.1*)

gambol NOUN frolic or play ❏ *Hop in his walks, and gambol in his eyes* (*A Midsummer Night's Dream 3.1*)

gaskins NOUN gaskins is an old word for trousers ❏ *or, if both break, your gaskins fall.* (*Twelfth Night 1.5*)

gentle ADJ gentle means noble or well-born ❏ *thrice-gentle Cassio!* (*Othello 3.4*)

glass NOUN a glass was another word for a mirror ❏ *no woman's face remember/ Save from my glass, mine own* (*Tempest 3.1*)

gleek VERB to gleek means to make a joke or jibe ❏ *Nay, I can gleek upon occasion* (*A Midsummer Night's Dream 3.1*)

gust NOUN gust meant taste, desire or enjoyment. We still say that if you do something with gusto you do it with enjoyment or enthusiasm ❏ *the gust he hath in quarrelling* (*Twelfth Night 1.3*)

habit NOUN habit means clothes ❏ *You know me by my habit* (*Henry V 3.6*)

heaviness NOUN heaviness means sadness or grief ❏ *So sorrow's heaviness doth heavier grow/ For debt that bankrupt sleep doth sorrow owe* (*A Midsummer Night's Dream 3.2*)

heavy ADJ if you are heavy you are said to be sad or sorrowful ❏ *Away from light steals home my heavy son* (*Romeo and Juliet 1.1*)

hie VERB to hie meant to hurry ❏ *My husband hies him home* (*All Well That Ends Well 4.4*)

hollowly ADV if you did something hollowly you did it insincerely ❏ *If hollowly invert/ What best is boded me to mischief!* (*Tempest 3.1*)

holy-water, court PHRASE if you court holy water you make empty promises, or make statements which sound good but have no real meaning ❏ *court holy-water in a dry house is better than this rain-water out o'door* (*King Lear 3.2*)

howsoever ADV howsoever was often used instead of however ❏ *But howsoever strange and admirable* (*A Midsummer Night's Dream 5.1*)

humour NOUN your humour was your mood, frame of mind or temperament ❏ *it fits my humour well* (*As You Like It 3.2*)

ill ADJ ill means bad ❏ *I must thank him only,/ Let my remembrance suffer ill report* (*Antony and Cleopatra 2.2*)

indistinct ADJ inseparable or unable to see a difference ❏ *Even till we make the main and the aerial blue/ An indistinct regard.* (*Othello 2.1*)

indulgence NOUN indulgence meant approval ❏ *As you from crimes would pardoned be,/ Let your indulgence set me free* (*The Tempest Epilogue*)

infirmity NOUN infirmity was weakness or fraility ❏ *Be not disturbed with my infirmity* (*The Tempest 4.1*)

intelligence NOUN here intelligence means information ❏ *Pursue her; and for this intelligence/ If I have thanks* (*A Midsummer Night's Dream 1.1*)

inwards NOUN inwards meant someone's internal organs ❏ *the thought whereof/ Doth like a poisonous mineral gnaw my inwards* (*Othello 2.1*)

issue 1 NOUN the issue of a marriage are the children ❏ *To thine and Albany's issues,/ Be this perpetual* (*King Lear 1.1*) 2 NOUN in this context issue means outcome or result ❏ *I am to pray you, not to strain my speech,/ To grosser issues* (*Othello*)

kind NOUN kind here means situation or case ❏ *But in this kind, wanting your father's voice,/ The other must be held the worthier.* (*A Midsummer Night's Dream 1.1*)

knave NOUN a knave was a common word for scoundrel ❏ *How absolute the knave is!* (*Hamlet 5.1*)

league NOUN A distance. A league was the distance a person could walk in one hour ❏ *From Athens is her house remote seven leagues* (*A Midsummer Night's Dream 1.1*)

lief, had as ADJ I had as lief means I should like just as much ❏ *I had as lief the town crier spoke my lines* (*Hamlet 1.2*)

livery NOUN livery was a costume, outfit, uniform usually worn by a servant ❏ *You can endure the livery of a nun* (*A Midsummer Night's Dream 1.1*)

loam NOUN loam is soil containing decayed vegetable matter and therefore good for growing crops and plants ❏ *and let him have some plaster, or some loam, or some rough-cast about him, to signify wall* (*A Midsummer Night's Dream 3.1*)

lusty ADJ lusty meant strong ❏ *and oared/ Himself with his good arms in lusty stroke/ To th' shore* (*The Tempest 2.1*)

maidenhead NOUN maidenhead means chastity or virginity ❏ *What I am, and what I would, are as secret as maidenhead* (*Twelfth Night 1.5*)

mark VERB mark means to note or pay attention to ❏ *Where sighs and groans,/ Are made not marked* (*Macbeth 4.3*)

marvellous ADJ very or extremely ❏ *here's a marvellous convenient place for our rehearsal* (*A Midsummer Night's Dream 3.1*)

meet ADJ right or proper ❏ *tis most meet you should* (*Macbeth 5.1*)

merely ADV completely or entirely ❏ *Love is merely a madness* (*As You Like It 3.2*)

misgraffed ADJ misgraffed is an old word for mismatched or unequal ❏ *Or else misgraffed in respect of years* (*A Midsummer Night's Dream 1.1*)

misprision NOUN a misprision meant an error or mistake ❏ *Misprision in the highest degree!* (*Twelfth Night 1.5*)

mollification NOUN mollification is appeasement or a way of preventing someone getting angry ❏ *I am to hull here a little longer. Some mollification for your giant* (*Twelfth Night 1.5*)

mouth, cold in the PHRASE a well-known saying of the time which meant to be dead ❏ *What, must our mouths be cold?* (*The Tempest 1.1*)

murmur NOUN murmur was another word for rumour or hearsay ❏ *and then 'twas fresh in murmur* (*Twelfth Night 1.2*)

murrain NOUN murrain was another word for plague, pestilence ❏ *A murrain on your monster, and the devil take your fingers!* (*The Tempest 3.2*)

neaf NOUN neaf meant fist ❏ *Give me your neaf, Monsieur Mustardseed* (*A Midsummer Night's Dream 4.1*)

nice 1 ADJ nice had a number of meanings here it means fussy or particular ❏ *An therefore, goaded with most sharp occasions,/ Which lay nice manners by, I put you to/ The use of your own virtues* (*All's Well That Ends Well 5.1*) 2 ADJ nice here means critical or delicate ❏ *We're good… To set so rich a man/ On the nice hazard of one doubtful hour?* (*Henry IV part I*) 3 ADJ nice in this context means carefully accurate, fastidious ❏ *O relation/ Too nice and yet too true!* (*Macbeth 4.3*) 4 ADJ trivial, unimportant ❏ *Romeo .. Bid him bethink/ How nice the quarrel was* (*Romeo and Juliet 3.1*)

nonpareil NOUN if you are nonpareil you are without equal, peerless ❏ *though you were crown'd/ The nonpareil of beauty!* (*Twelfth Night 1.5*)

office NOUN office here means business or work ❏ *Speak your office* (*Twelfth Night 1.5*)

outsport VERB outsport meant to overdo ❏ *Let's teach ourselves that honorable stop,/ Not to outsport discretion.* (*Othello 2.2*)

owe VERB owe meant own, possess ❏ *Lend less than thou owest* (*King Lear 1.4*)

paragon 1 VERB to paragon was to surpass or excede ❏ *he hath achieved a maid/ That paragons description and wild fame* (*Othello 2.1*) 2 VERB to paragon could also mean to compare with ❏ *I will give thee* *bloody teeth If thou with Caesar paragon again/My man of men (Anthony and Cleopatra 1.5)*

pate NOUN pate is another word for head ❑ *Back, slave, or I will break thy pate across (The Comedy of Errors 2.1)*

paunch VERB to paunch someone is to stab (usually in the stomach). Paunch is still a common word for a stomach ❑ *Batter his skull, or paunch him with a stake (The Tempest 3.2)*

peevish ADJ if you are peevish you are irritable or easily angered ❑ *Run after that same peevish messenger (Twelfth Night 1.5)*

peradventure ADV perhaps or maybe ❑ *Peradventure this is not Fortune's work (As You Like It 1.2)*

perforce 1 ADV by force or violently ❑ *my rights and royalties,/Plucked from my arms perforce (Richard II 2.3)* 2 ADV necessarily ❑ *The hearts of men, they must perforce have melted (Richard II 5.2)*

personage NOUN personage meant your appearance ❑ *Of what personage and years is he? (Twelfth Night 1.5)*

pestilence NOUN pestilence was a common word for plague or disease ❑ *Methought she purg'd the air of pestilence! (Twelfth Night 1.1)*

physic NOUN physic was medicine or a treatment ❑ *'tis a physic/That's bitter to sweet end (Measure for Measure 4.6)*

place NOUN place means a person's position or rank ❑ *Sons, kinsmen, thanes,/And you whose places are the nearest (Macbeth 1.4)*

post NOUN here a post means a messenger ❑ *there are twenty weak and wearied posts/Come from the north (Henry IV part II 2.4)*

pox NOUN pox was a word for any disease during which the victim had blisters on the skin. It was also a curse, a swear word ❑ *The pox of such antic, lisping, affecting phantasims (Romeo and Juliet 2.4)*

prate VERB to prate means to chatter ❑ *if thou prate of mountains (Hamlet 5.1)*

prattle VERB to prattle is to chatter or talk without purpose ❑ *I prattle out of fashion, and I dote In mine own comforts (Othello 2.1)*

precept NOUN a precept was an order or command ❑ *and my father's precepts I therein do forget. (The Tempest 3.1)*

present ADJ present here means immediate ❑ *We'll put the matter to the present push (Hamlet 5.1)*

prithee EXCLAM prithee is the equivalent of please or may I ask – a polite request ❑ *I prithee, and I'll pay thee bounteously (Twelfth Night 1.2)*

prodigal NOUN a prodigal is someone who wastes or squanders money ❑ *he's a very fool, and a prodigal (Twelfth Night 1.3)*

purpose NOUN purpose is used here to mean intention ❑ *understand my purposes aright (King Lear 1.4)*

quaff VERB quaff was a common word which meant to drink heavily or take a big drink ❑ *That quaffing and drinking will undo you (Twelfth Night 1.3)*

quaint 1 ADJ clever, ingenious ❑ *with a quaint device* (*The Tempest 3.3*) 2 ADJ cunning ❑ *I'll... tell quaint lies* (*Merchant of Venice 3.4*) 3 ADJ pretty, attractive ❑ *The clamorous owl, that nightly hoots and wonders/At our quaint spirit* (*A Midsummer Night's Dream 2.2*)

quoth VERB an old word which means say ❑ *'Tis dinner time.' quoth I* (*The Comedy of Errors 2.1*)

rack NOUN a rack described clouds or a cloud formation ❑ *And, like this insubstantial pageant faded,/ Leave not a rack behind* (*The Tempest 4.1*)

rail VERB to rant or swear at. It is still used occasionally today ❑ *Why do I rail on thee* (*Richard II 5.5*)

rate NOUN rate meant estimate, opinion ❑ *My son is lost, and, in my rate, she too* (*The Tempest 2.1*)

recreant NOUN recreant is an old word which means coward ❑ *Come, recreant, come, thou child* (*A Midsummer Night's Dream 3.2*)

remembrance NOUN remembrance is used here to mean memory or recollection ❑ *our remembrances of days foregone* (*All's Well That Ends Well 1.3*)

resolute ADJ firm or not going to change your mind ❑ *You are resolute, then?* (*Twelfth Night 1.5*)

revels NOUN revels means celebrations or a party ❑ *Our revels now are ended* (*The Tempest 4.1*)

rough-cast NOUN a mixture of lime and gravel (sometimes shells too) for use on an outer wall ❑ *and let him have some plaster, or some loam, or some rough-cast about him, to signify wall* (*A Midsummer Night's Dream 3.1*)

sack NOUN sack was another word for wine ❑ *My man-monster hath drowned his tongue in sack.* (*The Tempest 3.2*)

sad ADJ in this context sad means serious, grave ❑ *comes me the Prince and Claudio... in sad conference* (*Much Ado About Nothing 1.3*)

sampler NOUN a piece of embroidery, which often showed the family tree ❑ *Both on one sampler, sitting on one cushion* (*A Midsummer Night's Dream 3.2*)

saucy ADJ saucy means rude ❑ *I heard you were saucy at my gates* (*Twelfth Night 1.5*)

schooling NOUN schooling means advice ❑ *I have some private schooling for you both.* (*A Midsummer Night's Dream 1.1*)

seething ADJ seething in this case means boiling – we now use seething when we are very angry ❑ *Lovers and madmen have such seething brains* (*A Midsummer Night's Dream 5.1*)

semblative ADJ semblative means resembling or looking like ❑ *And all is semblative a woman's part.* (*Twelfth Night 1.4*)

several ADJ several here means separate or different ❑ *twenty several messengers* (*Anthony and Cleopatra 1.5*)

shrew NOUN An annoying person or someone who makes you cross ❑ *Bless you, fair shrew.* (*Twelfth Night 1.3*)

shroud VERB to shroud is to hide or shelter ❏ *I will here, shroud till the dregs of the storm be past* (The Tempest 2.2)

sickleman NOUN a sickleman was someone who used a sickle to harvest crops ❏ *You sunburnt sicklemen, of August weary* (The Tempest 4.1)

soft ADV soft here means wait a moment or stop ❏ *But, soft, what nymphs are these* (A Midsummer Night's Dream 4.1)

something ADV something here means somewhat or rather ❏ *Be something scanter of your maiden presence* (Hamlet 1.3)

sooth NOUN truly ❏ *Yes, sooth; and so do you* (A Midsummer Night's Dream 3.2)

spleen NOUN spleen means fury or anger ❏ *That, in a spleen, unfolds both heaven and earth* (A Midsummer Night's Dream 1.1)

sport NOUN sport means recreation or entertainment ❏ *I see our wars/ Will turn unto a peaceful comic sport* (Henry VI part I 2.2)

strain NOUN a strain is a tune or a musical phrase ❏ *and so die/ That strain again! it had a dying fall* (Twelfth Night 1.1)

suffer VERB in this context suffer means perish or die ❏ *but an islander that hath lately suffered by a thunderbolt.* (The Tempest 2.2)

suit NOUN a suit is a petition, request or proposal (marriage) ❏ *Because she will admit no kind of suit* (Twelfth Night 1.2)

sup VERB to sup is to have supper ❏ *Go know of Cassio where he supped tonight* (Othello 5.1)

surfeit NOUN a surfeit is an amount which is too large ❏ *If music be the food of love, play on;/ Give me excess of it, that, surfeiting,/ The appetite may sicken* (Twelfth Night 1.1)

swain NOUN a swain is a suitor or person who wants to marry ❏ *take this transformed scalp/ From off the head of this Athenian swain* (A Midsummer Night's Dream 4.1)

thereto ADV thereto meant also ❏ *If she be black, and thereto have a wit* (Othello 2.1)

throstle NOUN a throstle was a name for a song-bird ❏ *The throstle with his note so true* (A Midsummer Night's Dream 3.1)

tidings NOUN tidings meant news ❏ *that upon certain tidings now arrived, importing the mere perdition of the Turkish fleet* (Othello 2.2)

transgress VERB if you transgress you break a moral law or rule of behaviour ❏ *Virtue that transgresses is but patched with sin* (Twelfth Night 1.5)

troth, by my PHRASE this phrase means I swear or in truth or on my word ❏ *By my troth, Sir Toby, you must come in earlier o' nights* (Twelfth Night 1.3)

trumpery NOUN trumpery means things that look expensive but are worth nothing (often clothing) ❏ *The trumpery in my house, go bring it hither/ For stale catch these thieves* (The Tempest 4.1)

twink NOUN In the wink of an eye or no time at all ❏ *Ay, with a twink* (The Tempest 4.1)

undone ADJ if something or someone is undone they are ruined, destroyed, brought down ❑ *You have undone a man of fourscore three* (*The Winter's Tale 4.4*)

varlets NOUN varlets were villains or ruffians ❑ *Say again: where didst thou leave these varlets?* (*The Tempest 4.1*)

vaward NOUN the vaward is an old word for the vanguard, front part or earliest ❑ *And since we have the vaward of the day* (*A Midsummer Night's Dream 4.1*)

visage NOUN face ❑ *when Phoebe doth behold/ Her silver visage in the watery glass* (*A Midsummer Night's Dream 1.1*)

voice NOUN voice means vote ❑ *He has our voices* (*Coriolanus 2.3*)

waggish ADJ waggish means playful ❑ *As waggish boys in game themselves forswear* (*A Midsummer Night's Dream 1.1*)

wane VERB to wane is to vanish, go down or get slighter. It is most often used to describe a phase of the moon ❑ *but, O, methinks, how slow/ This old moon wanes* (*A Midsummer Night's Dream 1.1*)

want VERB to want means to lack or to be without ❑ *a beast that wants discourse of reason/ Would have mourned longer* (*Hamlet 1.2*)

warrant VERB to assure, promise, guarantee ❑ *I warrant your grace* (*As You Like It 1.2*)

welkin NOUN welkin is an old word for the sky or the heavens ❑ *The starry welkin cover thou anon/ With drooping fog as black as Acheron* (*A Midsummer Night's Dream 3.2*)

wench NOUN wench is an old word for a girl ❑ *Well demanded, wench* (*The Tempest 1.2*)

whence ADV from where ❑ *Whence came you, sir?* (*Twelfth Night 1.5*)

wherefore ADV why ❑ *Wherefore, sweetheart? what's your metaphor?* (*Twelfth Night 1.3*)

wide-chopped ADJ if you were wide-chopped you were big-mouthed ❑ *This wide-chopped rascal* (*The Tempest 1.1*)

wight NOUN wight is an old word for person or human being ❑ *She was a wight, if ever such wight were* (*Othello 2.1*)

wit NOUN wit means intelligence or wisdom ❑ *thou didst conclude hairy men plain dealers, without wit* (*The Comedy of Errors 2.2*)

wits NOUN wits mean mental sharpness ❑ *we that have good wits have much to answer for* (*As You Like It 4.1*)

wont ADJ to wont is to be in the habit of doing something regularly ❑ *When were you wont to use my sister thus?* (*The Comedy of Errors 2.2*)

wooer NOUN a wooer is a suitor, someone who is hoping to marry ❑ *and of a foolish knight that you brought in one night here to be her wooer* (*Twelfth Night 1.3*)

wot VERB wot is an old word which means know or learn ❑ *for well I wot/ Thou runnest before me* (*A Midsummer Night's Dream 3.2*)